THE POWER
TO CHANGE YOUR LIFE

THE POWER
TO CHANGE YOUR LIFE

A Step-by-Step Program for Planning Your Future

KATHRYN JASON
AND JOE McMAHON, Ph.D.

Doubleday & Company, Inc., Garden City, New York
1982

Originally published in Brazil as *A Coragem de Decidir*,
copyright © 1980 by Kathryn Jason and J. J. McMahon.

English language edition copyright © 1982 by
Kathryn Jason and J. J. McMahon
Library of Congress Cataloging in Publication Data

Jason, Kathryn.
   The power to change your life.

Translation of: A coragem de decidir.
   1. Success.   2. Values.   I. McMahon, J. J.   II. Title.
            BF637.S8J3513   158'.1
         ISBN 0-385-17736-4   AACR2
Library of Congress Catalog Card Number 81-43118

For
José Carlos Leal and Joanna and Aris McMahon,
whose love keeps us most attached to life.

CONTENTS

A Personal Note

Mini-fast. That is the trend people in search of a more fulfilling life find in the self-help field today. Mini-workshops. Mini-courses. Mini-books with fast solutions for complex problems. Instant happiness with the mini-techniques of fast-selling psychologies. Mini-chapters with mini-words covering issues so hastily that only a superficial understanding results.

Mini-thinking. That is what is encouraged in most self-help books today. Keep it simple; don't introduce complex ideas. Be concrete; don't be abstract. Keep moving at a pace that allows the reader to get excited about your topic, then move on to another before he or she gets bogged down by thinking. Just state a complex problem in mini-words, give a quick solution, and add a mini-fast pep-talk.

What results for the reader is a mini-"high" usually lasting a few hours, or at best a few days. At the end of that time, the reader is left wondering why his or her life still doesn't work.

A closer look at most self-help books reveals that they are simply pep-talks which do not encourage the reader to reflect about his or her life or examine his or her motivations or intentions in a meaningful, lasting way. Instead, the message seems to be "You're doing that? Wrong! Do this instead, and you'll be a success like me! You're feeling that? Wrong! Stop these feelings, and your life will be as happy as mine!" Anyone who has read such books knows that a real feeling of peace with oneself and fulfillment in life does not result from such superficial techniques or blanket answers.

A great part of what is being held out to the public today is nothing more than a defensive psychology that may at times lead to short-term self-profit (such as winning an argument or gaining power over those around you), but can never lead to the true nourishment of the human spirit that brings real growth and fulfillment.

While we may realize self-profit from such defensive psychology, we also cut off all honest, spontaneous feelings that bring beauty and growth to a relationship. By denying our feelings, we may give the appearance of being in control, but we are also left with the feeling of emptiness and alienation that is so poignantly prevalent in our society today.

An examination of some of these books that tell the readers to stop their feelings, to win at all costs, to intimidate others in order to protect themselves, reveals the shrinking soul of the Western man and woman. Though imbued with the mini-fast spirit of the times, these are not books that encourage harmony within ourselves or in our relationships with others. On the contrary, they exalt narcissistic self-profit through techniques for controlling others. Though presented convincingly and with a tone of grandiose optimism about our potential for control, these books leave readers with a feeling of alienation, defensiveness, and emptiness. It is no small wonder that this is so; for, in fact, these books are nothing more than catalogs of the authors' views of the booby traps that the world has set for us. They tell us how to "survive" and "protect ourselves," rather than how to co-exist creatively with those around us.

While the ideas of self-profit and hedonism have a great appeal for many readers, and though the subjects sell very well, they are simply not enough. The techniques presented in self-help books today are maps for moving from irrational confusion and dependency to rational control and order; and this indeed usually yields some benefit. But there is a step beyond, to the supra-rational, where a few lucky people find a sense of flow in life, a feeling of movement in harmony with themselves. This is the level of vision and creativity that leads to true self-growth and to contribution to others. It is the level at which a person feels free to *choose* his or her life.

It is our belief that many people today are seeking a vision of what is fundamentally important to them, rather than searching for the secrets of protecting themselves or intimidating others. We believe that they are also seeking more than techniques that may be helpful in some limited aspect of their lives, but leave them struggling with the same problem they faced when they picked up the book: *How do I find the* process *in life that results in the courage to move in whatever direction I choose?*

This book is about the process that leads to the courage to make decisions to change your life. Decision-making is, itself, a *living* process. *And it is a philosophical process as well as a psychological one.* In the following chapters, we illustrate the various phases of that process in order to help you to decide how you will experience the process of your own life.

Just what is this process that leads to the courage to make your life harmonious? How do you become most aware of your options, freer to choose those options, and make your life more satisfying? We present the process in three parts.

Part I: Discovering the Issue

This is a process of recognition of, and careful reflection about, the fundamental issues that cause you to stop short of realizing your full potential and enjoying where you are in life. It means examining those fears and weaknesses that prevent you from seeing your potential to move in whatever direction you choose.

Part II: Discovering Yourself

This is a process of understanding your own motivations and intentions so that you can make clear decisions about your life. It means examining how those motivations and intentions color what is important to you, and how your life will be an expression of your own values.

Part III: Discovering the System

This is a process of learning to take responsibility for where your life is at a given moment and of creating a disciplined system to move you toward positive change. It means awareness of your goals; examining all alternative paths to those goals; acknowledging the risks involved; considering people important to you; and finally, it means tapping your courage to choose. It means searching within yourself for the strength to freely choose the direction of your own life.

This book is written for those people who are willing to reflect on their own decisions in life instead of following a list of "shoulds" and "should nots." Its tone is different from the tone of many popular self-help books because it is not a pep-talk to excite you for the moment and to leave you empty later because it has failed to deal thoroughly with fundamental issues. Although we have stripped away the technical jargon of psychology and philosophy, as you read, you may recognize the insights of William James, John Dewey, Henri Bergson, Alfred North Whitehead, Sigmund Freud, Victor Frankl, Carl Rogers, Albert Ellis, and Alfred Adler, among others. Anyone familiar with pragmatism, process philosophy, client-centered therapy, and rational-emotive therapy will recognize the theories implicit in each chapter. We emphasize, however, that it is not at all necessary to know these philosophies or therapies to understand the decision-making process described in this book. We have begun where all philosophies and therapies begin: in personal experience.

We hope that the book will inspire you to reflect on your own life so that you will be better able to live the life that the deepest part of you desires. That life depends upon your courage to decide, then to act on your decision. This concept is beautifully expressed in the following poem, "The Ways," by John Oxenham.

To every man is open a way, ways, and a way.
And the high man takes the high road,
And the low man takes the low.
And in between, on the misty flats,
The rest run to and fro.
To every man is open a way, ways, and a way.
And every man decideth which way his path will go.

The following chart represents the choice that you face today. The answer to where the path will go is in the process. We do not offer you a bag of tricks or a repair kit for wounded egos. We offer you instead a process that will help *you* to discover your *own* techniques for living the process that is your life.

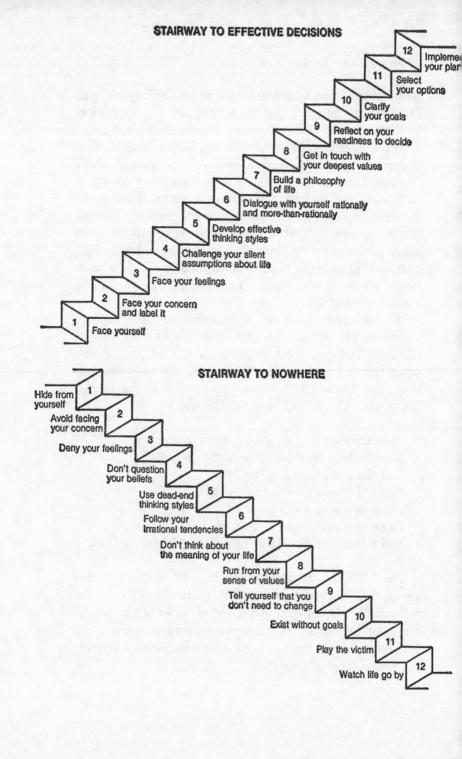

STAIRWAY TO EFFECTIVE DECISIONS

12 Implement your plan
11 Select your options
10 Clarify your goals
9 Reflect on your readiness to decide
8 Get in touch with your deepest values
7 Build a philosophy of life
6 Dialogue with yourself rationally and more-than-rationally
5 Develop effective thinking styles
4 Challenge your silent assumptions about life
3 Face your feelings
2 Face your concern and label it
1 Face yourself

STAIRWAY TO NOWHERE

1 Hide from yourself
2 Avoid facing your concern
3 Deny your feelings
4 Don't question your beliefs
5 Use dead-end thinking styles
6 Follow your irrational tendencies
7 Don't think about the meaning of your life
8 Run from your sense of values
9 Tell yourself that you don't need to change
10 Exist without goals
11 Play the victim
12 Watch life go by

PART ONE

DISCOVERING THE ISSUE

Chapter One

Do You Want to Change Your Life?

One of the most difficult realities of making positive changes in our life is that with every choice we make to move forward to something, we are simultaneously choosing to move away from something else. Most people feel this most painfully in love relationships or in career choices. When we choose to make a truly full commitment in marrying someone, for instance, we are also choosing to close off other romantic relationships that we might otherwise have experienced. It is no small wonder, then, that most of us feel ambivalence in fully committing ourselves to a romantic love relationship. In choosing something, we learn too painfully, we are giving up something.

And so it is in choosing our life's work. Most of us remember how, at a tender age, we had fantasies of a career quite different than the one we have today. Somehow each choice that we have made about our work has caused most of us to reject our earlier fantasies. The reasons we give are varied, but it is not at all unusual to hear a person reflect on his or her life in terms of past decisions.

"How different my life would be today if at certain critical points I had made different decisions," this person might say. Perhaps that decision was marrying or not marrying someone; pursuing an advanced degree; leaving the country in which he or she was born; or making a conscious choice to reshape his or her life at some point. It is everybody's life story: where we are today is tremendously influenced by the decisions we have made in the past.

While many people speak of life in terms of their own decisions, others say, "How different my life would be today except for the hand of Destiny. Can you imagine if my father had not died and left us penniless?" or, "Do you remember when I was so desperate and John (or Mary) came along? That was fate. It changed my life." Or, "I will never forget how my company going bankrupt caused me to reevaluate my values. It's as if I were destined to fail and suffer in order to understand what is truly important to me."

But, while that ominous force of Destiny has evidenced itself in every person's life, it doesn't determine the entire course of a life. Ultimately, we are left with the responsibility to shape our lives based on the cards that Destiny has dealt us. Part of that destiny, Sigmund Freud tells us, hinges on the first six years of life, when we are more or less victims of circumstance. Do those first six years determine the rest of our years? Are we victims of our parents and our early environment? Perhaps to some degree. *Our salvation seems to be, however, that by taking responsibility for who we are today we can limit the ability of past damage, past defenses, to decide our future. We do have the power to decide about our lives. And that power lies in the freedom of the mind to choose an attitude.* Regardless of our environment and our conditioning, we can set ourselves free. And the more psychologically free we let ourselves become, the more possibilities for fulfillment we see in our particular circumstances.

Is Your Life Just "So-so"?

How many days of the year do you wake up happy with your life? How often do you exercise, and take pleasure in, your power to choose the way that you experience each moment? When is the last time that you remember being enthusiastic with the idea that you have total responsibility for what happens to you that day?

Surprisingly few of us can count very many of those days. On the other hand, most of us can count high into the 365 days of the year that we feel dissatisfied. We remember all too well the many days that we feel disappointed that our lives ever managed to become so radically different from that wonderful fantasy we had when we were younger. And we hate even to mention how many days we feel the victim of our home life, or of some other person's control over us.

Why are most of us such poor decision-makers about our personal lives? How is it that so many seemingly intelligent, well-educated people end up leading painfully unsatisfying lives? The answers seem to be self-ignorance and fear. Unfortunately, our educational system has not introduced most of us to the search for self-understanding that is so important in making decisions. In fact, most school curriculums do not even include problem-solving, choice awareness, or decision-making.

With the lack of training that most people have in decision-making and self-awareness, it is no small wonder that so many people today are searching for answers in mini-seminars, gimmicky self-help books, or magazine articles with titles such as "Ten Quick Steps to Happiness."

While we all admire the individual who seems to move through life with an awareness of what is important to him, what life means to him, where he intends to go, and a facility for dealing with conflicts and decisions—all of which lead to a feeling of harmony in his life—most of us never quite learn to duplicate that ability. Instead, we keep searching for "Ten Quick Steps to . . ."

The Fundamental Secret

The individual who feels in harmony with himself gets his marvelous ability to enjoy life fully, not from a library of self-help books, or from learning a list of behavioral techniques to stop others from manipulating him, or by learning five rules for creating a "halo effect" so that people will like him immediately. Although these techniques may contain kernels of truth, they are merely a first-aid approach to life's problems, and they stop short of dealing with our life as a whole.

Just what, then, *is* the secret that such a person holds? *The secret is that this person has faced himself, and has moved forward from that self-knowledge.* Facing yourself means discovering what is important to you and realizing what fears are stopping you from living what is important to you. And then it means having the courage to overcome your fears and to pursue the things you hold important.

So easy? You know better. All those self-help books with lists of solutions to your problems have already taught you, if nothing else, that the full process of change is more difficult than simply doing a series of exercises. You yourself are the process that you need to understand if you want to direct the change in your life. To know yourself as someone in process means to see where you are now in terms of your personal growth, where you want to go, and how to make the change. When you realize this, you will be surprised how easy it is to choose decisions to fit your values instead of feeling that decisions about your life are thrust upon you by circumstance.

There is a tremendous difference between making decisions about your life when you feel they are more or less forced upon you and making decisions because you truly *choose* them. Choosing an alternative rather than feeling trapped into a decision is the difference between feeling in control of your life and playing the victim of circumstance. Even though most of us insist that we would like to be in control of our lives, surprisingly few of us are able to say that we don't feel the victim of circumstance to some degree.

The psychiatrist Victor Frankl speaks to this point in his book *Man's Search for Meaning*. In writing of his ex-

periences in the concentration camps of World War II, he
recalls:

> The camp inmate was frightened of making decisions
> and of taking any sort of initiative whatsoever. This
> was the result of a strong feeling that fate was one's
> master, and that one must not try to influence it in
> any way, but instead let it take its own course. In ad-
> dition, there was a great apathy, which contributed
> in no small part to the feeling of the prisoner. At
> times, lightning decisions had to be made, decisions
> which spelled life or death. The prisoner would have
> preferred to let fate make the choice for him. The es-
> cape from commitment was most apparent when a
> prisoner had to make the decision for or against an
> escape attempt. In those minutes in which he had to
> make up his mind—and it was always a question of
> minutes—he suffered the tortures of Hell. Should he
> make the attempt to flee? Should he take the risk?

We are not suggesting that most of us can compare our
feelings of anxiety in decision-making with those of people who suffered the horror of the concentration camps of
World War II or, more recently, of the Vietnam War.
However, the basic characteristics of decision-making
that Frankl mentions here are those that each of us can
identify with in our own conflicts in decision-making at
times. See if you have experienced these feelings in making major decisions in your own life:

(1) Fear

(2) Feeling out of control of the situation

(3) Apathy

(4) Lack of commitment

(5) Emotional suffering

(6) Ambivalence about taking responsibility for an action

(7) Ambivalence about taking a risk

You have probably experienced some of these feelings when you have tried to improve the quality of your life by making a major decision. At times, some of us have the sensation that Frankl had as a prisoner: that the decision is a matter of self-survival. In Frankl's case, it was the question of physical survival; in our case it is often the question of the survival of the real self over the Social Face. If the self, as far as we can know it, is to survive, a decision must be made to make changes in our lives to nourish the conditions for growth. This means making decisions based on more than short-term self-profit.

The subject of self-profit brings to mind a friend we'll call Steve Evans. Most likely you have known someone like this in your own life. Steve made a major decision which brought him success in terms of money and prestige, but he seemed to be more unhappy afterward than before. Steve had discovered that though money and prestige can be very satisfying, they alone do not bring real harmony to a person's life. He has not considered his life goals and values, and he has opted for money and prestige rather than the deeper, more fundamental things that bring true contentment. In his particular case, that money and prestige were achieved by a line of work that conflicts with Steve's image of himself and his place in the world. He hates the work he has chosen solely to achieve what he thought he wanted, prestige and wealth. And instead of deep reflection to resolve his feelings of emptiness and depression, he drowns himself with work by day and with alcohol by night.

Decisions about our life, we see from Steve's experience, involve more than striving for what many people in our society see as "success"—money and status. If they are to be fulfilling, these decisions must also involve our view of the world, our view of our place in that world, and our considerations about the people close to us. Finally, they come down to the courage to choose. It is a challenge that many of us never face. But it is a challenge that, if met, will allow you to experience life with the greater control and freedom that each of us secretly dreams of.

How to Decide to Decide

Find a quiet, comfortable place to sit. Think for a moment of each person, issue, or thing that consumes significant moments of your life. Perhaps you are thinking of loved ones; of your superior or subordinates at work; of a competitor; of a goal you have; of skiing or boating or some other leisure activity; of commuting; or of financial obligations.

Now take those persons or things and list each of them on a sheet of paper. Next, place a plus sign beside those things or people that at this moment you have no desire to decide about. Possibly, this indicates that you feel satisfaction, and perhaps even fulfillment, with these aspects of your life now. Possibly, too, it indicates that you are not aware of a lot of possibilities for improvement there. As we continue, you can *decide* about that!

Next, place a minus sign beside those people or things that you decide you need to take some action concerning. This indicates that there are areas of tension, incompleteness, or dissatisfaction here that you already recognize.

Take another look at your list. Have you played safe? Have you deliberately left off some persons or things because you don't want to have to deal with deciding about them now? Have courage! Write down everything, and later you still can decide not to decide, if that is what you want.

You may find some of the following on your list:

Financial concerns	Sex
Children	Religion
Spouse	Self-development projects
Parents	Shopping
Friends	Driving the children to
Sports activities	activities
Television	Sleeping
Job	Eating
Fantasies	Thoughts about yourself
Reading	Commuting
Health	Worries and fears
Loneliness	

Or, of course, your list might be totally different.

Now choose from your list one person or thing about

which you would like to consider making some major decision.

Please keep in mind here, and throughout this book, that the actual activity of writing these things down is crucial to your developing your decision-making powers. Writing helps you to be accurate and concrete, and having your thoughts on paper allows you to refer to them later on.

Six Insightful Questions

To better understand this area of tension that you would like to make some decision about, you will find it helpful to answer the following questions:

1. WHAT: is going on in this area of your life today that is dissatisfying? And WHAT were *your* specific behaviors that allowed this situation to exist? (You may think of others' behaviors that also brought about this situation, but at this point focus only on *your* responsibility.)

2. HOW: do you know that this area of decision is the true source of dissatisfaction, rather than a symptom of another, more important problem?

3. WHEN: did you first notice a dissatisfaction?

4. WHY: do you think your life will be better if you decide to make a change in this situation?

5. WHO: is ultimately responsible for your life and the choices you make in your life?

6. WHERE: do you see a difference in circumstances, environment, and yourself now that causes you to feel a need for change that you haven't felt before?

There are no "right" answers for these questions except for number 5. You, of course, are the only person who can ultimately accept responsibility for your life and your decisions. If you are accustomed to having a spouse, therapist, friend, or parent make decisions for you, then only you are responsible for the choice to let them do that. If you have spent your life avoiding major decisions because you fear you might choose wrongly, then you have, in fact, been *making* decisions: you have decided not to decide. Even your very indecision is a decision.

The function of the above six questions is simply to help you to put into perspective the tension area about which you would like to make a decision. Let's take a closer look at these questions.

1. By understanding specifically WHAT is dissatisfying in your life and WHAT specific behaviors of yours allowed that situation to exist, you can get a better view of what you feel is wrong and what you can do to prevent the situation in the future.

2. HOW do you determine that the area for decision is the true area of dissatisfaction, rather than a symptom of another more important problem? Let's suppose that you have chosen "spouse." You may think, for example, that your spouse does not treat you well—or at least not the way you would like him or her to treat you. Perhaps you would like to make a decision to do something about your spouse's attitude. But isn't this treatment by your spouse, in fact, a symptom of something more important? Doesn't it indicate something that *you* have been doing to allow

this problem to occur? This realization, then, brings the responsibility for what is happening back to *you*. It encourages you to look at yourself and your own behavior and decide how *you* can communicate more openly and assertively about your own rights and self-worth. The decision, then, begins to encompass a change in you and your spouse's communication with one another. We do not mean to suggest, however, that recognizing your responsibility in making a relationship work is necessarily going to make that a satisfying relationship. There are times when the other partner has such an investment in his or her attitude that even though *you* change the way you are communicating with him or her, he or she does not move an inch. That is probably when you will decide to begin to move away from the relationship.

3. WHEN did you first notice a tension? As you reflect on that initial pain of tension, you will clarify to yourself what value of yours was being challenged at that moment. Identifying this threatened value is the first step toward reducing the unproductive tension you're feeling now.

4. WHY do you think your life will be better if you decide to make a change in the situation? By reflecting on this question, you may be better able to judge if the decision is one that will truly improve the quality of your life. If, after considering it, you don't anticipate any significant improvements, perhaps you will prefer to choose to change an area of more importance to you. Are you playing safe by choosing an area that is not very significant to you anyway?

6. WHERE do you see a difference in circumstances, environment, and yourself that causes you to feel a need for change that you haven't felt before? Do you find a

change, for instance, in the way you respond to things happening around you, to your physical setting, or to yourself? Noting this difference is simply one more step to self-awareness that will help you make clearer decisions.

If you find that the outcome of your decision depends on another person's response (such as your spouse changing his or her attitudes), we suggest that you recast your decision so that the outcome is solely in your hands. While people close to you clearly may color the situation as it now stands—and you may indeed perceive them to be the *cause* of the problem—the responsibility of the decision must be *yours*.

We urge you again to *write down* your responses as you read each chapter. You may be quite surprised when you reread them after you have finished the whole book.

Chapter Two

So What's Holding
You Back?

Just how do you meet this challenge of deciding to change
your life? How do you increase your feeling of harmony
in life? First by increasing your self-understanding, and
second by acting on that understanding. One of the first
steps in understanding the fears that keep you from making positive changes in your life is to pay attention to
your feelings as you think of making a decision. By examining the following psychological characteristics that
Victor Frankl mentions in *Man's Search for Meaning*,
you may begin to get a clearer picture of some of your
own feelings.

Fear

Nothing is so shattering to efforts to change your life as fear. Many people do not make major decisions to change because, when they *do* see the possibility of change, they are immobilized by fear of the risks involved. "What if I fail? What if I lose the security I have now? How will I deal with all the problems my family will create about the change? What if I lose their love because of my decision? Maybe I'd just better forget the whole idea." Some fear is natural, of course, when you are considering a major change, but if you are immobilized by such thoughts, you opt for having fear control your life.

Realistic fear is a feeling of apprehension, a universal human experience generated by the anticipation of physical or emotional threat. Realistic fear is protective and useful, in that it warns us to avoid things that will hurt us. Unrealistic fear, on the other hand, is destructive.

For example, if you should hear on the radio today that an earthquake is expected in your city, it is most likely that you will experience realistic fear: your home and your life may be threatened. However, if you experience fear every time you think of walking out of your house when no disaster has been forecast, you are experiencing unrealistic, debilitating fear.

Unfortunately, many people have never learned to overcome their fears because they have been socialized to believe that if they admit fear, they will be perceived as weak. They have become masters of speaking and behaving in ways to hide their fears from others and of convincing even themselves that they are fear-free. And thus they often lose sight of what they feared in the first place, and seething anxiety takes over where fear once stood.

A noted characteristic of anxiety is the inability to identify the *source* of apprehension, and for this reason anxiety, contrary to realistic fear, is destructive. It is difficult enough to deal with apprehension when we *know* what we are afraid of; but when we lose sight of the *object* of our fear, we lose our ability to control that fear. We cannot truly control something that we can't even identify.

Perhaps in your own efforts to change your life, you are aware of what makes you afraid actually to take the necessary steps. If so, you are in touch with your fear. A useful exercise for you at this moment is to write down your fears so that you can see the impact they are having on your decisions as you work through the program.

On the other hand, you may be afraid of something you can't pinpoint; you may have an anxiety that you are unable to explain. If you are living with anxiety, you will most likely have noticed some of the following symptoms. Take a moment to check off which of these symptoms you identify in yourself:

irritability	sweating
tension	stomach discomfort
excessive urination	poor concentration
rapid heartbeat	fatigue
dry mouth	high blood pressure
broken sleep	frequent headaches
hyperventilating	

While these are more commonly noted symptoms of

anxiety, you may have others that are peculiarly yours. Some people, for instance, report to have nervous twitches when they are anxious; others lose the circulation in their legs. The noted theologian Paul Tillich has said that the fundamental anxiety of human existence is the anxiety of death. We are hardly born before we are aware of one certainty: death. Our finiteness is frightening to most of us, and yet we do not often focus on it. Instead, the fear of dying often becomes a mysterious anxiety that colors our behavior and hampers our desire to make positive changes in our lives. Change becomes another threat of the unknown, the ultimate of which is death.

Another anxiety that has been studied in depth in our society is the anxiety of meaninglessness. Dr. Victor Frankl's logotherapy is based on the theory that one of man's greatest anxieties results from the feeling that nothing has meaning. This perceived lack of meaning leads to, "I'm not here for any reason; *I* don't have meaning: my life is insignificant; *all* life is insignificant." As we will see in later chapters, discovering a meaning for your life will help you feel less anxious and will create a framework for changing your life.

If anxiety is keeping you from changing your life, perhaps by the time you have read the last chapter of this book you will have a better sense of what makes you feel anxious. If not, it may be helpful for you to speak to a competent counselor or psychotherapist in order to locate the source of that anxiety which is a major hindrance to healthy decision-making—and therefore a major hindrance to a satisfying life.

FEAR OF THE UNKNOWN

One of the major fears that people express to us in our work in decision-making is fear of the unknown. All of us experience fear of the unknown at times, but we manage to control our nervousness and keep our eyes on our goal. Other people, however, are paralyzed by fear of the prospect of a new job, a new apartment or house, a decision about business ventures, or even of going to a party where they don't know any of the other guests. They are afraid of the unknown. If you are one of these people, you can expect tremendous loss of opportunity in your life.

If you are aware of specific fears that you face every time you think of changing your life, jot them down as you think of them. As you look at them in print, try not to be judgmental about having these feelings. Remind yourself that they simply *are*. They exist. By *accepting* these feelings instead of judging them—and yourself—cowardly, stupid, or ridiculous, they begin to lose their power. By taking this more objective look at your fears, you will find that you begin to see more clearly whether the fear is useful to you, and can begin to find the freedom to move beyond it.

Often, people who are afraid to make major decisions don't seem to be in touch with what is involved if they *don't* change their lives. As we said in the opening chapter, the painful aspect of decision-making is that when we choose one thing, we are simultaneously choosing to *give up* another. However, just as there are costs in changing, there is a price in deciding not to change your life. Reflect for a moment about some major move you would like to make in your life now. What is the pain and feeling of loss that you experience in *not* making a change? Isn't there, in fact, as ominous a risk involved in *not* having the courage to choose as there is in actually choosing?

Feeling Out of Control

If, in the face of making a major decision, we have a feeling of control and certainty, we usually feel comfortable about taking that decision. However, the complexity of life itself defies complete certainty, and therefore any effort to improve our life must result in a certain amount of ambiguity. But lack of 100 percent certainty is quite different from feeling out of control. We can understand how Victor Frankl's subjects—concentration-camp prisoners—often felt that their lives were truly in the hands of destiny and that they had no control over what might happen to them. Even in normal life situations, however, many people adopt that same attitude: what will be, will be.

If you are at a point where you feel that you are not freely choosing to be where you are in life, think for a moment of the desired change(s) you would like to make. Write them down, and then do the following exercise that Leon did.

Leon is a young man of thirty-two who was living in the suburbs of New York City when he came to us for counseling in decision-making. We asked him to state his conflict, as simply as possible, on a sheet of paper. He responded, "I have always dreamed of being a vice-president or president of an engineering firm. However, the firm I chose to work for after I left the university has been taken over in the past year by another firm, which is owned by two families, the Beschers and the Manors. My prospects for becoming an officer of the company are dim because the company is now family-run. Since the Bescher and Manor families know the personnel director at the only real competitor in our town, I don't know whether to apply at the competitor or just resign myself to being a manager at Bescher-Manor. If I'm not accepted by the competitor, the personnel director may reveal that I tried to get a job there, and then I'll be on the outs at Bescher-Manor. For the first time in my life, I'm afraid that I've lost control over determining my own future."

If, in the face of a threat, we feel unable to control the probable outcome, we will almost certainly experience fear. However, most of us can exert far greater control over our lives than we recognize, as Leon later discovered.

We asked Leon to break down the things he had written to indicate that he was out of control of his destiny. He wrote the following:

1. My company has been taken over by two families.

2. They prefer that the officers in the company be family members.

3. They know Higgens, personnel director at the competitor.

4. Higgens may not hire me.

5. Higgens may tell Bescher-Manor that I'm looking for work.

6. Bescher-Manor may be offended and try to get rid of me all together.

Then we asked Leon to make a list of how he might *still* be able to control his advancement, but he was feeling so pessimistic that he couldn't find an answer. With encouragement from us, however, he finally came up with the following list:

1. Perhaps I could propose enough outstanding ideas that Bescher-Manor would want me as an officer anyway.

2. I could research the exact positions at the competitor to know exactly if the job I am qualified for is available, and reduce my chances of being rejected.

3. I could begin looking at firms outside my area that offer more opportunity.

4. I could, over time, build up good enough relations with our present clients that perhaps I could have my own firm in five or ten years, and carry some of our clients or their recommendations with me.

(The list was later expanded as Leon became more comfortable with this sort of brainstorming.)

At this point, Leon began to realize that he had more control over his life than he'd thought, and he began to feel the veil of apathy and depression lifting. Though this was only a small beginning in his decision-making process, he at least was beginning to have a positive attitude about his possibilities; his self-confidence began to return.

If you feel out of control of a situation in your own life, you are most likely feeling lack of self-confidence and self-esteem; for it is impossible to feel positive about yourself when you feel like a pawn being moved regardless of your own wishes. By taking the one small step of examining the possibilities that await you if you are just willing to work for them, you will begin to feel your self-confidence rise.

Apathy

Apathy is like a slow-killing cancer: it eats away at life and leaves an ugly corpse. Apathy is usually thought of as indifference or lack of interest; but more often than not, apathy represents feelings that have been cut off or awareness that hasn't been tapped. When does a person so totally cut off his or her feelings that he or she goes through life with an overriding sense of apathy? Usually when he or she believes that events are uncontrollable and that he or she is therefore helpless. Apathy seems to be closely tied to the feeling of being out of control. The apathetic person usually accepts his life as if there were no room for change or growth. Many of us have been socialized to believe that there is virtue in accepting our "lot," as if Destiny had handed us a life about which we had little to say. People in this category hold the attitude, "Well, I guess that's the way my life is supposed to be." If you are one of these persons, you probably find yourself justifying where you are in your life at this moment in terms of what your parents or society "did" to you; in terms of the "station" in life you were born into and therefore will always remain in; or in terms of how presumptuous you would appear if you broke out of the constraints of your surroundings and made radical changes in your life. You opt for having others make decisions *for* you, and you rationalize that what you are doing is "accepting" life. While this attitude is contrary to the Great American Dream and is diametrically opposed to the position of our cultural hero Horatio Algier, it is an attitude held by a surprisingly large number of people.

Then there is the more "scientific" explanation of why you are what you are. Believing that you are just the result of your genes and environment, you may live out the idea, "What will be, will be. Why put so much time into making decisions about things beyond my control?" Consider that viewpoint as you apply it to other people. If you have ever complained about the actions of others, then you were assuming that they could have behaved differently. That assumption negates the fatalistic, "What will be, will be" philosophy. If you expect others to exert their will to change, you can at least expect the same of yourself.

While it is true that fate, chance, or circumstance may indeed play a profound role in life, we do always have the power to decide how we will experience what happens to us, or how we will change our "lot" in life.

Lack of Commitment

It is not surprising that those of us who do not feel a strong commitment to a person, goal, or ideal find it difficult to make major life decisions. To commit oneself to something means to bind oneself to a certain line of conduct; to pledge oneself. In order to feel commitment to anything, we must first be intensely aware of a value we hold. What is important enough to make us want to move toward it, to bind ourselves to it?

Each of us has known someone who never seems to make commitments, and usually a person who is conscious of this attitude in him- or herself will say that lack of commitment is the safest way to play. This way, they argue, they leave all their options open. The sad ending for people who play out this reasoning in their life, however, is that all they have is options. They never make the choice to be intensely involved with or devoted to anything or anybody, and they usually find themselves wondering why they feel so fragmented.

If you feel that your own obstacle to making positive changes in your life is a lack of commitment, you will find Chapter Seven, "Values: The Compass of Your Mind" helpful in reconciling this problem.

Emotional Suffering

Making a major change in your life will always bring a degree of stress, and at times, emotional pain. The fact that you are very clear about both your goals and how you will achieve them does not ensure lack of emotional suffering along the way. However, our own observation of people we have counseled and trained in decision-making leads us to believe that the amount of emotional suffering you will experience throughout a major change will be inversely proportional to (a) how clear you are about your own values and self-image, (b) how responsible you have been in preparing the people important to you for the change, and (c) how carefully you have prepared yourself to meet the challenges you will meet in your new situation. All of these aspects will be dealt with in the following chapters.

EMOTIONAL INVESTMENT IN IMAGE

One of the dominant reasons for emotional suffering in making radical changes such as leaving a conventional, "acceptable" vocation (engineer, doctor, lawyer, teacher) to pursue a less conventional vocation (actor, artist, model, psychic healer), or to divorce after many years of marriage, is concern about not only how other people will view you, but how you view yourself. Peter Mortin's case illustrates this problem.

Peter is a young man with a wife, Laurie, and two children. Peter married Laurie because she was very pretty, a lot of fun, and very easy to be with. Twelve years later, however, Peter feels that he has continued to grow in his personal awareness and that Laurie has not. Also, since shortly after their marriage he has felt that Laurie is not a very nurturing person, and this has caused him much concern. Very often he feels that the relationship is empty, and he finds Laurie's understanding of his feelings very shallow. The "fit" of the relationship feels different today than when he took his marriage vows.

Peter thinks he has gone through the process of deciding to divorce Laurie. He has felt the tension and dissatisfaction in the marriage, and has told himself that he must leave the relationship. After all, he thinks, isn't that what everyone else seems to be doing these days when a relationship is no longer satisfying?

However, something keeps holding Peter back. And of course, until he actually *moves* on his decision, it is not a true decision. It is merely a thought. Finally, Peter realizes that he takes no action because, while he is unhappy with Laurie and sees no real hope of his ever feeling fulfilled in their relationship as it is, he says to himself, "I see myself as a loyal husband and father; I'm an upstanding member of the community, and everyone sees me as a person of commitment and trustworthiness. What will the neighbors think of me if I leave Laurie? And that son-of-a-bitch Bradley on the board of directors. I don't have the proper company image, he'll say. Besides, I don't like to think of myself as uncommitted and untrustworthy. How could I once feel such a full commitment to Laurie and now not feel it? Maybe I don't understand what commitment is." Peter is suffering true emotional pain and conflict. He thinks he knows what he wants, but does he want it badly enough to risk having people view him as less conventional and acceptable than they do today? Part of Peter's suffering and indecision stems from not being clear about what he values and the price he is willing to pay for it.

Peter, then, like many of us, is back at the point of decision-making that requires an understanding of our self-image and our values. He may eventually work the problem out himself, or he may seek out a skilled counselor to help him clarify his values and his self-concept. If you feel that you suffer from indecision because of fear of how others will view you, you will want to read Chapter Seven very carefully.

CONCERN FOR PEOPLE IMPORTANT TO YOU

Another reason for emotional suffering in making a major decision is anxiety over the consequences for others involved. For instance, our friend Peter thinks he wants to dissolve his relationship with Laurie. However, he is frustrated by wanting to maintain an image of himself as a loyal and trustworthy individual who is an upstanding member of the community. But his conflict is *further* complicated because he cares for his wife and children, and he feels they will experience great emotional damage if he leaves the family. Thus, his own desire for a more compatible mate is mitigated by guilt that such an action would hurt the persons important to him. Peter now has the problem of not only trying to take a new look at his self-image and his values, but he also has to consider his belief that his decision to leave will damage others. He may talk himself into believing that he must sacrifice his own happiness for his wife and children, or he may consider how he can leave the family while continuing to give them emotional support and while undertaking family counseling sessions to work through emotional conflicts. He may also begin looking at possible ways to change the marriage so that he *can* be happy living with his family. (You can follow Peter's story in later chapters.)

Preparing to Meet the Challenges

Another cause of emotional suffering in decision-making is a feeling of helplessness. "I'm miserable; I want to change," we may say. And yet if we don't feel *prepared* to change, we begin to feel helpless. It is a feeling that is all too common among people who are struggling to better their life: they are not aware of requirements for attaining their goals or of other alternatives for which they might be better prepared. And finally, if they manage to *reach* their goal, these people may not be emotionally prepared to meet the challenges of the new situation. Thus, the price of change seems too high.

If you sense this tendency in your own decision-making, this book will show you how to break that pattern.

Reluctance to Accept Responsibility

Responsibility is a big word. With it comes obligation and accountability. Many people avoid responsibility by reasoning that without responsibility, they are free. But there is a tremendous mistake in this thinking—for with freedom *comes* responsibility. The truly free person is one who assumes complete responsibility for his or her own life, and thus freely chooses the direction of that life.

To assume that responsibility, however, means giving up blaming others for where we find ourselves in life. It means taking time to reflect about what is most important to us, so that our life will reflect that value. It means commitment and a certain psychological stability. With this in mind, it is no small wonder that so few people are willing to make that word "responsibility" an important part of their pursuit of happiness. And yet the rewards of accepting the fact that a full life means a responsible life are tremendous. By simply accepting our primary responsibility in life—the responsibility to determine our own direction, our own happiness—we already begin to set ourselves free: free of guilt from dependence on others; free of resentment toward others for "failing" us; free of fear to choose. This book has been written to aid people who are searching for how to begin to accept that liberating responsibility.

Reluctance to Take Risks

Whether or not you are willing to take the necessary risks to change your life is a matter of courage, a subject which we will deal with in depth later in this book. Each of us faces a certain amount of nervousness in the face of the unknown. And yet, if we are not willing to struggle past those fears, the only significant change in our lives (besides growing old) will be regression instead of progression.

Calculated risk-taking is a necessary ingredient in decision-making; and as you will see in later chapters, the more fully prepared you are for possible risks, the more satisfied you will be with the choice for change that you make in your life.

Is one of these seven psychological characteristics—fear, feeling out of control, apathy, lack of commitment, emotional suffering, reluctance to accept responsibility, and reluctance to take risks—keeping you from making an important decision in some area of your life right now?

Unfortunately, most of us do not realize that *the power to decide about our life is the essence of freedom.* Even a prisoner of war, who is truly a victim of circumstance and by all appearances at that moment has no control over his life, is able to make a decision: to decide upon his *attitude* toward his lack of physical freedom.

In decision-making, it is essential that we become aware of our own attitudes and feelings. By delving into those ideas and feelings, where they originated, and whether or not they are helpful to us, we are better prepared to make decisions about our life. Part Two will treat this aspect of the decision-making process, which is fundamental to making effective decisions for change.

PART TWO

DISCOVERING YOURSELF

Chapter Three

The First Step

Understanding Past Decisions

How well do you understand the decisions you have made in your life? How well do you know your motivations—the things that propel you toward or away from something—and your intentions—the goals you desire? Many people explain their decisions by saying, "I just felt it was the right move for me," or "I just knew intuitively that that was what I should do." As we will see in later chapters, this can, in fact, be a good reason to make a decision; for intuition is often a reliable aid to decision-making.

Many people, however, don't have the slightest idea of what motivated them to make certain crucial decisions. They seem to end up in places that they never had any intention of being, and they have no idea how they got there.

Understanding your decisions means understanding *yourself*. To know ourselves means to be in touch with our deepest feelings of hope, joy, anxiety, frustration, creativity, and a host of other vital vibrations that we experience in our daily encounters with life. Every day that we grow in knowledge of ourselves, we are discovering a new dimension of our mind. The mind, so complex and often so deceiving, is a beehive of mental energy. Are you aware of how your mind deals with rejection? With pain? With sorrow? With joy? The more we get in touch with the power of our mind, the more we realize that we have only scratched the surface in knowing ourselves. Socrates urged his students to know themselves because he knew that the most exciting, fascinating, and rewarding research possible was exploring the depths of our own being. There, in your own mind, is the secret of your own personal power and of your ability to decide about your life.

Our dissatisfaction with our life decisions results from not knowing ourselves at the deepest levels of our existence. When we take hold of ourselves at the root of our being—that is, when we are aware of our deepest feelings and thoughts about our life—we draw on our vital energy. *Making decisions means directing this vital energy into those actions that will make us feel most alive.*

In Chapter One, you identified those areas of your life that concern you immediately. If you want to decide to do something about one or more of those parts of your life, you need to grow in knowledge of yourself before you begin to set goals. In this chapter, you will take the first step toward better decisions by understanding how your feelings affect your decisions.

Defining Yourself in Your Decisions

Your decisions are a statement of who you are. Decisions are not isolated "things" on the periphery of your life; they *are* your life. Your decisions are not isolated from the roots of your being; they *are* your being. Every decision that you make reflects what you think and what you feel. Each decision of your life reflects how you view yourself and your relationship to your world. You may at times have difficulty dealing with this concept. "I had no choice," you might say. "I didn't understand the consequences." "It wasn't my fault." "I know I did that, but it doesn't have anything to do with my real character; it's an isolated event." "I just didn't know enough at the time."

And yet, the fact remains that the decisions you make are who you are. Understanding who we are is not an easy undertaking. It means getting in touch with our deepest thoughts and feelings, which few of us do. You say you know your thoughts and feelings? Have you ever tried writing down for one complete day, every thought and feeling you have? It means non-stop writing, of course. And you can't even write that fast. If you are able to do it for only a few hours completely honestly, you will find material for tremendous insight into yourself.

Fortunately, such an exercise is not the only way we have of examining what goes on in our mind. You can reflect on your thoughts and feelings sporadically throughout the day to try to stay in tune with your truest self.

What is important is that you pay attention to what you think and feel in order to understand who you are and what is of meaning to you. Only then are you likely to be happy about the direction your life takes as a result of your decisions.

A surprising number of people think that they know themselves "inside out." Carolyn was one of these people. She constantly made critical remarks about her friends who seemed at times confused about their motivations or desires.

At the age of thirty-two, Carolyn was preparing for her third marriage. If you had met her six months before and asked her what caused her two divorces, she would quickly list the inadequacies of her former husbands. Having rejected both these men, she was looking forward to a better life with "Mr. Right."

Carolyn became extremely irritated when her mother suggested that before she take her vows again, she should examine her own self to understand the other side of why her marriages were failures. "Don't be ridiculous," she retorted. "I know myself inside out. I don't need to examine *anything*." By feeding herself this line, of course, Carolyn was on a path of not knowing herself at all.

A few months later, Carolyn was in a state of panic. The marriage date was drawing nearer, and suddenly she began to find fault with everything about "Mr. Right," down to the way he brushed his teeth. She came home to her mother one day crying, "I don't know what's happening. I thought he was so wonderful, but right now I don't like *anything* about him. I'm scared to death to get further involved with him."

It was at this point that Carolyn, with her mother's help, began to understand a side of herself that she had never dared take a look at. Carolyn was, in fact, "scared to death" to get deeply involved in a relationship with *any* man. She was fortunate to have a perceptive mother to help her understand that, actually, she had broken both her previous marriages just at the point that she was beginning to feel emotionally involved in a significant way. While she kept the relationships light and superficial, they survived; however, when the men began to ask for more emotional involvement and true commitment, she withdrew. "Mr. Right" had been ready for a truly deep involvement earlier than her two husbands had, and for that reason she panicked *before* the wedding rather than *after*.

Carolyn, obviously, had not known herself "inside out," as she had thought. It took her several months of therapy, in fact, to begin to understand *why* she feared deep involvement with another person. It seems that her father, in his own sadness in life, had never paid much attention to her when she was a child. Therefore, she had learned early that to be emotionally attached to a man and to be rejected by him was an incredibly painful experience. And when her father died in her early adolescent years, she found that loss of a man she loved left her with a desperate feeling of helplessness. Her subconscious rationale: Don't ever get deeply attached to a man again, because he's going to reject you and leave you.

Once Carolyn started to examine her thoughts and feelings with a skilled therapist, she began to create a more meaningful life for herself. Instead of merely treating the symptoms of her problem, she took hold of it at the root, by examining her deepest thoughts and feelings.

Recognizing Your Self-defeating Feelings

Like Carolyn, we have all at one time or another done something without understanding what hidden emotional rumblings were motivating our behavior. We feel compelled to move in the direction that these covert feelings are pushing us, even when our mind recognizes the danger of letting those feelings, such as anxiety, inadequacy, or hate, determine a decision.

Although it is indeed dangerous to let these negative feelings determine a decision, it is also dangerous to react to them as if they were our bastard children. Our strong desire to ignore these emotions because they bring up feelings of confusion and pain blinds us to their presence at times. But no matter how much we try to ignore these unwanted feelings, we can never annihilate them by pushing them out of consciousness.

Although our feelings and thoughts occur simultaneously, we are usually more aware of our feelings initially, especially in critical moments. Suppose you are thinking about making an important decision that may radically change your life. Feelings of anxiety may gush up so quickly that what you thought was cool-headed consideration is drowned in a flood of mixed emotions. Because feelings are indicators of thoughts, and because we are often more conscious of how we feel than what we're thinking, we'll examine the role of feelings before that of thinking.

The story of Jean will illustrate some of the ways that

feelings can prevent us from making those decisions that will contribute to our growth.

Jean is thirty-five years old, divorced, and a mother of two children, a fifteen-year-old boy and a thirteen-year-old girl. For the past five years, she has been holding down a modest-paying secretarial position. Now she is thinking about beginning college on a part-time basis in order to prepare for a career in the medical field—perhaps as a nurse. As Jean looks to the future and assesses her present situation, she experiences a host of mixed feelings. Notice the feelings that Jean is avoiding as she speaks.

"I'm thirty-five. It's now or never. I think I know enough about my abilities to make a career decision. The results of my career test supported my strong desire to go after a position in the medical field. My high school grades and aptitude test results tell me that I have the ability to succeed. Now I have to get started. But it's been so long since I've done any kind of academic work! Suppose I find the work too much? And I still have to take care of my kids. Suppose I fail? For the past fifteen years I've been kept down. That's what he was trying to do to me all the time, keep me down. Oh well, I suppose I could continue in my present job indefinitely. It has good benefits, and as the years go by I'll get my raises. And it will leave me more time with the children. If I keep my eyes open, maybe I can get a promotion and become an administrative assistant. At any rate, I can begin to take classes in night school. I'll see what happens. If things go well, I'll take courses leading toward a nursing degree."

Jean's words reveal deep feelings affecting her decision. In the first part of the dialogue she feels *hopeful* as she appraises her interests and abilities. In the middle of her dialogue the sharp edges of *fear of failing* cut into her awareness. After she reflects on her concern for her children, some *anger* toward her former husband surfaces. At this point she looks at the alternative of staying in her present job, which now seems to have some appeal to her. At the end of the dialogue she seems to have *lost her determination* to pursue a career in the medical field and now feels that she should only "take some classes." She skirts the challenge of facing the negative feelings rumbling under her conscious self-assessment. She feels inadequate. She feels afraid. She feels her husband must have been right about her. Instead of paying attention to these feelings, however, Jean searches for some positive aspects of her present job and points to her children with feelings of caring.

The affection is most likely sincere; however, Jean uses it to escape her fear. The fear of failing has significantly influenced Jean's choice. Both the quality and the quantity of her options have been limited. She will choose only those classes in which she will probably succeed, even though they do not prepare her for a career in medicine. Jean protects herself from the feelings of fear, but she also misses the opportunity to deepen her self-confidence and to grow in the direction she truly prefers. She weakens her power to change her life by not reflecting on her fear and not struggling to overcome it. She does not recognize her self-defeating patterns.

Facing Your Feelings

How many times have you submerged your anger for so long that finally you exploded in a fit of rage? Andy has that experience about once a month with his wife, Judy. Judy henpecks Andy daily, and he usually ignores it, until he finally can't stand it any longer. Then he throws things, yells until the neighbors are disturbed, and calls his wife filthy names. About once a month Andy lets his feelings run away with him.

Our feelings usually run away with us when we ignore them too long. If Andy would deal with each henpecking remark that his wife made and help her examine her motivation in doing this, he wouldn't need to lose control of his feelings. He would be in control of his feelings by dealing with them the moment he first felt irritation.

When we lose control of our negative feelings, they usually result in an *explosion*—rage—or an *implosion*—depression. Rage is uncontrolled anger turned outward, while depression is uncontrolled anger turned inward. Think about the times you lose control of yourself in rage or depression. Aren't all of these moments the result of not dealing with a problem the moment it reared its ugly head? Dealing with problems and feelings the moment they occur is all part of the process of deciding to make your life better.

What do you do about your feelings of fear, anxiety, sadness, joy, or others that you have? First of all, you must "own" these feelings; you must recognize that they are yours. That is more difficult for some of us than most people ever imagine. Next, you must examine where these feelings came from and whether it is still appropriate for you to hang onto them. Once we are ready to relinquish some of our feelings that, while once appropriate in a different context, are no longer productive, we can move on to new experiences and new decisions with an openness to deal only with what *is* rather than what *was*.

Listening to Your Feelings

A crucial point in deciding to change your life is in listening to yourself and examining what you are thinking and feeling. Listening to your feelings means: 1) you accept their *presence* in you; 2) you accept the *statement* that they might be making about you; and 3) you accept the *questions* that they might raise about you.

Perhaps you have had the experience of watching someone who was obviously furious about something—slamming doors, knocking things over—and you have said, "Gosh, I'm sorry you're so angry about what I did. Don't you think we could talk about it?" only to have the person answer, "Angry? Who's angry? I'm not angry. It's not important. There's nothing to talk about." Now, perhaps this person *knows* he's angry and just doesn't want to talk about it. But very often this behavior comes from a person who has convinced *himself* that he's not angry because what is at the bottom of all that anger is hurt. The mind will do many things to avoid emotional pain, and one of those things is to push painful awarenesses into the subconscious where they rumble around, waiting to be dealt with, popping up in all sorts of strange circumstances, running people's lives in indirect ways so that they don't even understand their own behavior. It happens to all of us: we simply refuse to listen to many of our feelings because they are uncomfortable and often threatening.

Accepting Your Feelings

Just how do you go about accepting your feelings? First, you must concentrate on those inner rumblings. How often do you pay close attention to what you are feeling? For example, when you feel depressed because someone you love has rejected you, if you are paying attention to your feelings you can describe to yourself what is going on inside you. You might say, "I feel as though I'm falling apart. I'm crumbling into a heap. I feel hurt, I feel in pain." Getting in touch with your negative feelings is not a pleasant experience, but it is definitely a helpful one. Recognizing feelings is the first step toward dealing with them. And by dealing with those negative feelings, you develop a deeper understanding of yourself and can move forward from depression or anger.

Accepting the Statements Your Feelings Make About You

By moving from accepting the presence of your feelings to questioning what statements they make about you, you begin to get a clearer picture of who you truly are. This may not sound like such an earthshaking idea, but it is something that very few people do in life. Never understanding their own feelings, most people muddle through, wondering why their life never gets any better. Most often, their life isn't getting any better because they are not listening to themselves at the deepest level and discovering what really brings meaning and joy to their life. "Oh, yeah," you may say, "my problem is different. I've already discovered that money will bring meaning to my life, but I don't know how to get it." The interesting thing is that when people *truly* discover what brings them a sense of fullness in life, they somehow manage to go after it. It's only when we don't have an idea of what is meaningful to us that we are immobile. If money is what you think will bring you fulfillment in life, and you aren't devoting your full attention to getting money, then in your deepest self money is *not* a prime motivator. You simply haven't searched carefully enough for what *is* meaningful to you. You need to listen more carefully to your feelings about yourself and what makes you feel most alive.

Accepting the Questions Your Feelings Pose

We do not propose that this acceptance is an easy task, for people never know themselves completely. But by acknowledging, "This is the way I'm feeling," and asking, "What does that say about me? When did I begin feeling this way? When did I have a similar experience that made me feel like this?" you begin to develop insights into yourself and begin to understand how your past experiences are coloring your present experiences through your unconscious. That simple awareness opens up a host of new choices to you in deciding how to change your life.

Trusting Your Feelings

Trusting your feelings is necessary in order to make positive changes in your life. When we say that you ought to trust your feelings, we are not suggesting that you move on every desire or whim that you feel. As a matter of fact, nothing could be more harmful to positive movement in your life than acting impulsively on momentary feelings.

Trusting your feelings means that you stay in touch with what you are feeling in order to responsibly think through what those feelings are indicating about your conscious and subconscious evaluations.

The feeling you must trust above all is the deep feeling of freedom that all of us have experienced at some moment. Because we often fear our freedom and the responsibility that naturally comes with it, we frequently try to avoid it, as Eric Fromm has so comprehensively explained in his book *Escape from Freedom*. When we refuse to trust our ability to direct our own lives, we can no longer accept the responsibility of making decisions. We would rather have others tell us what to do. If, on the contrary, we believe that our freedom is pushing us in the direction of human fulfillment, then we will listen to these feelings as we make decisions concerning our personal growth. *The most important message is that we freely choose to be the person we are.* Our freedom, then, is the centerpiece of our personality. No authority except our own prevents us from thinking whatever we decide to think, even though we sometimes might be alarmed by the thoughts and feelings that run through our minds because they are so uncharacteristic of the image that we have of ourselves.

If you do not trust the freedom of your mind to make prudent judgments about significant changes in your life, try the following exercise:

1. Recall a situation in which you decided to do something important to you, and afterward felt good about your choice of action. Perhaps it was going back to school, changing your job, getting married, moving to a different city, losing ten pounds, breaking off a relationship, apologizing to someone, going into therapy, or making a full commitment to something or someone. We can all find at least one decision that has satisfied us. The event that you remember may appear insignificant in the eyes of other people; nevertheless, you are the only person who knows why a particular choice of yours is so important.

2. Review that decision in slow motion by asking yourself the following questions:

    a. At what point did I know I had to make a change?
    b. What was I thinking and feeling that helped me make the decision?
    c. What did I consider to be important to me?
    d. What consequences did I expect from my decision?
    e. How did I feel at the moment that I actually accomplished the act that I'd decided on.

The purpose of this exercise is to help you learn the art of listening to yourself. You have the power to see what is important to you and the power to choose a course of action that is a visible expression of your values. Remembering the effective decisions that you have made in the past is a way of awakening these powers and stimulating yourself to have the courage to change your life again.

At this point you might want to take an inventory of all the feelings that you experience whenever you think about making a decision in some area of your life. Remember that you can direct your feelings to your own advantage if you permit yourself the freedom to explore all of them in depth. Following is a list of some feelings that you might experience. Try comparing the intensity of your positive feelings with that of your negative ones as you try to make a decision about some area of your life. For example, if you are thinking about changing your job, you might be experiencing greater feelings of despair than of hope, or of frustration than of patience.

despair	frustration
hope	patience
fear	hate
courage	love
sadness	doubt
joy	trust
anxiety	guilt
peace	self-acceptance
anger	
assertiveness	

If you feel immobilized by your negative emotions, you are being self-defeating. Your feelings don't just appear from out of the void. Whether you are aware of it or not, your thoughts determine those feelings. We do not intend to give you six quick steps for cutting off those feelings or stopping those thoughts. Rather, we encourage you to *own* those feelings and thoughts, and to examine where they came from through a process of self-reflection. Certainly, this is more difficult than repeating, "I'm not going to feel inferior anymore. It's getting me nowhere. I'm the greatest," to yourself in the mirror every morning. But how often has that really *worked* for you in your life? What happens when the pep talk, a momentary painkiller, is over? A feeling of well-being is not sustained by taking a painkiller every morning, but comes from the courage to examine your deepest thoughts and feelings about your own life and to find your direction therein.

In the next chapter, we will examine the types of thinking that affect your feelings and prevent you from choosing effectively, as well as the modes of thinking that will help you to decide your own direction.

Chapter Four

Have You Noticed
How You're Thinking Lately?

Identifying Your Assumptions

When you are in the process of making an important decision, many silent assumptions are guiding your thinking. Take a good look at several false assumptions that many people make. How many of them are determining your own choices?

FALSE ASSUMPTION #1:   *To live is to cope.*

If your fundamental question each day is, "How can I cope with my life?" "How can I get through this day?" or "How can I just maintain things as they are?" you are assuming that to live is to cope. Coping is something that we all have to do at times, but there is nothing more dull or more dehumanizing than to spend your days coping.

People who only cope with life are like swimmers who only tread water. They avoid drowning, but they never really go anywhere.

Do you spend your life treading water, or do you enjoy the exhilaration of free-style swimming? If you are a treader, you maintain a position but never take great risks.

Have you ever tried instead the assumption: *To live is to see and actualize your values?*

When you live your values—put first priority on things that are genuinely most important to you—you change your attitude from one of coping to one of fulfilling yourself. You stop choosing things that preserve the status quo and instead choose things that propel you forward. Jim, for instance, is a young man of thirty-five who recently had a bad case of stomach ulcers. He hated his life as a salesman, and usually spoke in terms of "coping" with things. And, indeed, that was what he was doing. He was holding a high-pressure sales job with an engineering firm because he earned more money that way, but what he really wanted to do was get out to the sites and get his hands on the project itself. His wife, however, tended to be a big spender, and he felt that he had to hold onto his sales job in order to finance her shopping sprees.

When Jim recognized that his ulcers were caused by the stress of working at something that was not most important to him and by his wife's problem with overspending, he went with his wife for family counseling. After several weeks of tension and upset, Jim resolved his problem: he is now an engineer, and his wife is working part time to earn her spending money. Jim no longer has to cope with the stress of a job he hates. And he no longer has to cope with his wife's problem—he has allowed *her* to assume responsibility for that.

FALSE ASSUMPTION #2: *You can get rid of negative feelings forever.*

Many people today are perplexed by self-help books perpetuating the idea that we shouldn't have negative, self-destructive feelings. These books list various techniques and strategies to accomplish this, and readers are left wondering what is wrong with them when it doesn't work. Maybe you have tried some of these techniques. When you have felt guilt, anger, hate, hostility or anxiety, you may have used the technique of telling yourself, "This isn't rational. I will not allow this self-destructive thought into my mind." It may not be rational, but the answer is not in denying the feeling or thought outright.

Have you ever tried assuming: *to live is to allow yourself the freedom to experience your feelings and go beyond them to experience new feelings and new insights?*

This is not an easy challenge. But if you want to change your life for the better, you must deal with the process of your thoughts and feelings. You must examine what you think and feel and why you think and feel that way, and you must make your own choices about how you want to move forward from these negative thoughts or feelings.

A young woman named Louise attended a lecture by an author of a popular book about getting rid of negative feelings. She felt exhilarated when she left the meeting. "I'm not going to feel mistrustful of men anymore," she told herself. "It's irrational and self-destructive. I'm going to start trusting the next man I date." Three weeks later, after telling herself every day, "It's stupid of me not to trust him. I can't allow myself to distrust him," she felt like a failure because the technique wasn't working: she still didn't trust him.

Louise will only begin trusting men when she examines painful experiences she has had even as far back as childhood to discover how she began to hold the belief, "I can't trust a man." When she *understands* the experience and sees that it has no bearing on her life today, she will take the first step toward trusting people who demonstrate that they are trustworthy.

FALSE ASSUMPTION #3: *The world is only what you perceive it to be (or, perception is reality).*

One popular "human potential" figure tells his followers that "there's nothing out there. All reality is subjective. You create your reality." Is that so?

Graham was a young man who left one of these lectures feeling fantastic that he was responsible for his own reality, and that his reality was not necessarily someone else's. Graham perceived himself as an excellent, efficient, office manager. On Monday when he reported to work, he found that his boss was less appreciative. "Graham," he said, "I'm not pleased with the way this office is being run. Tremendous time is being lost by lack of proper planning. I want to see some changes made."

Graham, proud of his new philosophical insight, replied, "I understand that's the way you perceive the situation, but my perception of the situation is my reality, and I don't think any changes need to be made."

He was astonished when his boss retorted, "You can

take your reality someplace else, friend. Have your office cleared by five o'clock."

Have you ever tried the assumption: *The same world is out there for all of us, but we each respond to it in a unique way?*

We *do* make our own reality in that we choose what attitudes we will hold and how we live our lives. What we do with the life that Destiny gives us is our individual reality. But to assume that reality is totally subjective only serves as a wonderful copout for not communicating with your spouse, lover, children, friends, or co-workers. "Well, that's just your perception of the problem," you can say. "My perception is something else, so I guess we just can't discuss the matter." To make the assumption that the world is only what *you* perceive it to be is to make your life decisions very lonely ones.

The practical way to test your perceptions is to check the consequences of acting on them. If you, like Graham, are adamant about the validity of your perceptions, only to find that they are self-defeating, you'd best go back and check your perceptions.

FALSE ASSUMPTION #4:   *Only the present counts.*

It is not uncommon to hear people say, "I don't care about commitments I've made in the past. I can't make commitments for the future. Only the here and now exists. Nothing else counts." When you observe the desperate lives these people lead, you see the results of this assumption. Frantically trying to break with responsibilities of the past and trying to avoid the discipline it takes to build for the future, they say, "I can't involve myself with those things. Only *right now* exists. I just have to enjoy this moment."

Have you ever tried the assumption: *Our present is based on what we have learned from the past and in turn determines our future?*

While it is true that you cannot (literally, at least) live in either the past or the future, it is very destructive to try to block out your memory of the past or your vision of the future. By assuming that only now counts, you do not leave yourself open to reflect on lessons from the past or to make choices to prepare for the future. Your living a full life *does* depend on how you live in the present. If you live only with sentiments of the past or daydreams of the future, it is impossible to do anything constructive in the here and now. Living a full life depends on your willingness to value the past in order to give added meaning to your present, as well as living the present moment in a way that will give meaning to your future.

FALSE ASSUMPTION #5:   *Realistic thinking is fact thinking.*

How often have you avoided a major change by telling yourself, "The fact of the matter is, that's just the way things are. And that's that." That may be the way things are, but who says they have to *stay* that way?

Fact thinking is often rationalized as "realistic" thinking. For example, Linda looked at the "facts" of her own unhappy marriage. Constantly abused by her husband, she said, "I want to leave him. But the fact is, I have no money of my own. So that's that. The only realistic thing for me to do is stay."

Have you ever tried the assumption: *Realistic thinking*

is analyzing and interpreting the facts in light of what is important to you?

While fact thinking is not realistic thinking, it *is* the *objective* component of realistic thinking. When we add the *subjective* component, we look at the facts in terms of what is important to us, what we are feeling, and how we can draw conclusions from these facts to improve our life.

When Lee began psychoanalysis, he was a fact-thinker. His analyst helped him to see that the reason that he had such a strong need to dominate his children, his wife, his employees, and his friends was that, as a neglected child, he felt as though he had no control over his own life. Shifted from boarding school to boarding school, Lee felt himself the victim of domination from every direction. As an adult, he overcompensated for this feeling of helplessness by trying to control others.

Lee's response at first was, "Well, that's just a fact. I *was* neglected. And I *did* hate not being able to get what I needed. And now I finally have control."

Gradually, his analyst helped Lee to realize that the thing he'd wanted most in his childhood was love. And what was he *feeling* about the dominating control he had over others now? Was it satisfying to him when it caused so much resentment from others? As Lee interpreted the facts in terms of what he really wanted most—more than success or prestige—he realized that it was not control over others that he really wanted today, but caring from others. By going beyond the bare facts in that way, Lee expanded his thinking and began to have more satisfying relationships. While he still exercises control in appropriate situations, he has given up his extreme need to dominate others.

In trying to change your own life, are you considering

the facts in light of what you feel, and in light of how you can change your life *despite* the facts?

FALSE ASSUMPTION #6: *You should set standards by comparing your life to others'.*

One of the most common mistakes people make in trying to change their life is to watch what others of their economic or social status are doing. In your own life, do you find that when several neighbors get a new car, you must have the latest model also, to indicate that you are as successful as they? Or if several of your friends enroll their children in a private school because it is the currently "chic" thing to do, are you compelled to do the same? And when everyone takes a cottage at the beach for the summer, do you rush to follow them even when you'd prefer to spend some quiet weekends in your own home? Or when a new club opens with outrageous membership dues and you have other priorities for your money, do you feel you must follow your friends and join anyway?

By basing what you do and what you have on what others do and have, you are indirectly allowing others to make decisions *for* you.

Have you ever tried the assumption: *Your life is fuller when you direct it according to your priorities and your feelings?*

Anna is a middle-aged woman who lives in South America. At forty-five, she finds her life empty because her husband is a high-powered businessman, her children have left home and have active lives of their own, and she has nothing to do each day except to go to social functions and give orders to her servants.

Actually, Anna would like to be an interior decorator. She has a wonderful flair for interior design, but she dares not become a "working woman," because that is not considered an acceptable thing for a woman of her social class to do. Her husband is astonished to learn that she is entertaining such thoughts, and says to her, "Haven't I provided well enough for you? Don't you have more than any of your friends have? What do you expect me to do when I need you to entertain my guests at a luncheon and you are out fighting with a bunch of painters? What will our friends say when they hear you are doing such a thing?"

By comparing Anna's life to her friends' lives, by comparing his wife's standards of fulfillment with his friends' standards, Anna's husband cleverly controls her ambition to have a career. "You must conform to the standards set by people of your social level," is the message he is giving her. With this message, Anna continues to live a life dictated by others rather than by herself. She remains frustrated because she does not have the courage to break out of conventional standards and begin a career for herself.

Whose standards are you living by? Do you fail to change your life because of the pressures exerted by other people to have you live a life that is convenient to them but unsatisfying to you?

FALSE ASSUMPTION #7: *You must conform to your role in life.*

In considering changing their lives, a surprisingly large number of people think in terms of their roles. "What would a good mother do in a situation like this?", Mrs. Carpenter asks herself when she is unsure whether or not to return to work now that her child is in the first grade. Mrs. Carpenter's idea of a good mother may have come from her mother's idea of a good mother, and her mother's idea of a good mother may have come from *her* mother's idea of a good mother, and so on and so on. And their ideas may be outmoded today. But Mrs. Carpenter, wanting to conform to the role of a "good mother," will most likely not return to work, and will instead become a frustrated housewife, resentful of her husband and child, and yet convince herself that she is a "good mother" because she is staying at home with her child.

Role-playing of a different kind is being promoted tremendously today by self-help books telling women how to be successful in the business world. "Don't forget your role," these books say. "Remember, you are a manager now. A person in your position should not have lunch with another female who is only a secretary. And don't be heard accepting a personal telephone call from a man during office hours. Your role is that of a businesswoman, not a social butterfly." Message: "Your competency is only a small part of the issue here. You must conform to your role in life."

Young women are not the only people pressured by role image in the business world. Corporate executives are also under tremendous pressure in this area and often get caught up in role-playing when choosing their personal lifestyle.

John Hart, for instance, is a senior vice-president of a major securities firm. Earning well over $300,000 per year, he feels he must conform to his role of a Wall Street broker in a three-piece suit and wing-tipped shoes. When John is at a party, he itches to get out on the dance floor and try the latest dances, but he is concerned that someone might think that is not fitting for an executive of a securities firm. He never releases spontaneous feelings on the tennis court because that's not the way an executive should behave, he tells himself. He balks at the idea of riding a bicycle at the beach with his teenagers because someone may say that he is not "serious." Despite his unhappy marriage, he dare not divorce his wife because he thinks it's not the proper image for a future director of his company. Meanwhile, his wife is having an affair, and he is dreaming of one. John Hart's real self has become lost in his role. The changes he makes in his life will be determined by how they accommodate his executive image.

Have you ever tried the assumption: *Your awareness of your possibilities expands more each day that you view yourself in totality rather than in a role?*

The more freedom you allow yourself to be the person you really feel like being, the more choices you have for your life. Ed was twenty-two years old when he graduated from the university in pre-law and announced that he was going to spend his life painting. "An artist!" his mother wailed. "But you can't be an artist! You have to take over your father's law firm!" The role of lawyer was not the role that Ed wanted to play. In fact, the role of *artist* was not the role Ed wanted to play. Ed was not interested in playing any role; he simply wanted to paint what he felt about the world. In viewing his work this way, he progressively felt more creative and free. He did not concern himself with his role either as a rich lawyer's son or as an artist. He concerned himself only with how he could best express himself, and he dedicated himself to that.

Take a moment to look at how you express yourself in

the world. Is it as someone's wife, husband, or parent? As an executive, jet-setter, teacher, or athlete? Are your decisions to change based on a role you are playing rather than on your total self awareness?

FALSE ASSUMPTION #8:   *Every decision is either/or.*

Remember the last time you said, "Okay, either I stay in this lousy situation or I leave"? If you really want to broaden your options for change, you will not indulge in either/or thinking. In general, people who rush into a solution by offering themselves only two choices lack either the insight to appreciate the complexity of the issue or the patience to handle that complexity. "I must either accept my marriage as it is or get a divorce." "I must fire this employee or have a disaster on my hands." "I must go to Harvard because Father went there, or Duke because Mother went there." This type of thinking closes the mind to new information and prevents it from seeing other possibilities.

Have you ever tried the assumption: *A decision is more satisfying when you search for many options and weigh them carefully?*

Seldom is a decision so limited that it demands a strictly either/or solution. Either/or thinking has its place, but only after we have allowed ourselves to be open to the full process of resolving an issue. By thinking that life changes must be made on an either/or basis, we limit our creativity in finding an answer. How many times have you made a decision by listing *all* the possible options and carefully weighing the consequences you expect from each?

FALSE ASSUMPTION #9:   *Your life is a mess because of other people.*

Blaming others for where they are in life is a favorite pastime of many people, and it is something that almost all of us do occasionally.

"I'm forty-five years old, and my life is a mess because my wife left me. There's just no hope for me to be happy again."

"I'd love to lead a more orderly, harmonious life. But it's impossible in my business."

"The only reason I'm not successful in my business is that my father doesn't give me an opportunity."

"If I had been born rich, I wouldn't be so miserable all the time."

Have you ever tried the assumption: *You are responsible for your own life?*

While others may color the way your life goes, the course of your life depends on your willingness to accept full responsibility for yourself and your actions in a given circumstance. You say your wife is making your life miserable? Who is allowing that? Your subordinates never get their reports in on time? Who lets them get away with it? You have no satisfaction in your life? Who, ultimately, is choosing that for you?

By catching yourself each time you indulge in victim thinking, you can remind yourself that you alone can accept responsibility for your decisions.

Open-ended Thinking

Probably the greatest stumbling block preventing us from making wise choices is not knowing how to use our mental powers. No matter how much we desire to change an aspect of our life, we will most likely remain just where we are until we learn the mental skills required to make effective changes. The following is a list of some of the mental skills used in effective decision-making. How many do you use when you try to make an important change in your own life?

Observe	Analyze and synthesize
Concentrate	Hypothesize
Perceive	Verify hypothesis
Recall	Choose options

1. How well do you *observe?* In making a major change in your life, you must observe yourself and the situation with all its possibilities if you want that change to be a satisfying one. Seems simple, doesn't it? And yet, very few people do it well. Take Herman Teal, for instance. He has been the Vice-President of the Engineering Group at a major communications corporation for eight years. His position, however, does not satisfy Herman's ego need to be in the limelight, and he has been struggling for years to become Vice-President of the Sales Group. Constantly criticizing the current Vice-President of Sales, Herman submits weekly reports to his superior to demon-

strate how he is doing the sales work that the Vice-President of Sales should be doing. He gossips with other employees about the incompetency of his rival and groans about what a tragedy it is that their competitor is going to take all their business away. He rushes to sales meetings to take the platform and explain, from an engineering point of view, the flaws of the current sales program. He spends hours collecting information on what the competitor is doing and leaves his collected data on his superior's desk to demonstrate that the Vice-President of Sales is unaware of the competitor's movements.

Herman Teal is puzzled that his tactics to change his work life are not working. Herman has not observed very well. He has failed, first, to observe *himself*. Caught up in his goal to take the job of Sales Director from someone else, he has not noticed that his ambition is only for his personal gain and not the company's. His backbiting tactics are destructive to the work atmosphere, as are his insinuations that the company is in a downtrend.

He has also failed to observe that his superior is concerned about Herman's health; for Herman has recently had a heart attack, and a stressful position such as Vice-President of Sales is not one for a man with such a condition.

Herman has also been so insensitive that he does not realize that people do not respond well to him; most people simply do not *like* Herman. Always groping to be the center of attention, he offends people by his overbearing personality and sarcastic comments.

As Vice-President of Engineering, Herman does not have to sell his own personality, as he would as Vice-President of Sales, and in fact he is very competent in his current position. His superior has no thoughts of making him

Vice-President of Sales. But Herman keeps beating his head against the wall, determined to get the position he wants. Only when he begins to *observe* himself and his situation will he see that he is caught up in a web of self-defeating frustration.

2. How well do you *concentrate?* Concentration means focusing your mental energy on what is most important to you in the present situation and on how you can achieve it.

Ruth, for instance, is terribly bored in her life in a small town in the Midwest. She talks incessantly of how she would like to move to Chicago, or maybe even New York. Excitement and adventure are what Ruth says are important to her, but she fails to concentrate on a strategy to get out of Dullsville. Most likely, Ruth will be in the same town ten years from now, complaining about her life, but always failing to *concentrate* on the specifics that would help her change it.

"What can I do to put some excitement in my life?" she should be asking herself. "How can I get that?" Instead, Ruth plays bridge most nights after working all day as a medical laboratory technician, goes out occasionally with some of the men from the local paper mill, with whom she shares no common interests, and dreams about the exciting life she reads about in *Vogue* and *Cosmopolitan*.

Do you find in your own desire to change your life that you spend more time daydreaming or complaining than you do concentrating on how to achieve your goal?

3. How well do you *perceive?* To fully perceive means to be intensely aware of the object we are sensing. There is a vast difference between hearing music and being wrapped up in it; between watching a play and in feeling that you are one of the characters; or between listening to

a person and in experiencing for the moment what he or she is experiencing.

Chuck, for instance, is a man in his early forties who has marvelous perception about business matters, but does not perceive other people's feelings so well. While he often finds himself quite lost in concentration on a business matter, able to see every angle of the situation because he involves himself so completely in what he is doing, he is totally unable to appreciate how his wife is feeling about things. He may listen to Susan and seem to be considerate and attentive, but he does not involve himself with her and her feelings the way he involves himself with his work. As a result, Chuck is unaware that when Susan says to him, "You know, it makes me feel very lonely that you're always so preoccupied when you come home," or, "I feel very sad when I try to tell you about some project I feel excited about and you always manage to turn the conversation back to one of your business problems," that she is really saying, "I'm not happy in this relationship. I feel lonely and rejected."

So involved in his own goals, Chuck fails to perceive how Susan feels. He also fails to perceive that their marriage is in trouble.

Do you allow yourself to deeply perceive another person or situation? If there is depth in your perceptions, you will be better able to make prudent judgments about the changes to be made in your life.

4. How well do you *remember?* Most of us have very selective recall. The angry or resentful lover begins to remember only the negative aspects of a relationship, for instance, because this selective memory supports his or her position that he or she is justified in being angry or resentful.

George is a thirty-eight-year-old man who is constantly changing his life, and unfortunately, seldom for the better. He has been married three times and remembers very well what he believes to be injustices inflicted on him by his three wives. He has held five jobs in the last ten years and remembers vividly the incompetence of his superiors that he reports as the reason for his frequent job changes.

In fact, George does not remember very well. He does not recall his demeaning comments or inconsiderate acts that caused his wives to withdraw from him to the point that he left them. Nor does he recall his inability to accept authority that caused his superiors to encourage him to look for employment elsewhere.

George's changes in his life result from an inability to make relationships work, but he is so determined to be "right" that he refuses to remember all of the circumstances that cause him to be constantly rearranging his life in unsatisfying ways.

How you go about changing your life depends greatly on what you are bringing to the present from the past: in other words, your memory. In trying to make decisions about your life, do you allow yourself to remember both positive and negative aspects of the situation you are trying to change in order to make a wiser decision? Do you try to recall with perception and understanding how things came to be the way they are?

5. How well do you *analyze* and *synthesize* your observations? In making decisions to change your life, whether you realize it or not, you go through a period of analysis of the situation. That is, you take the problem apart and spread all the pieces in front of you, whether mentally or on paper. If you have concentrated and perceived adequately in the past, and if you remember well at this mo-

ment, you should be able to analyze the problem completely.

However, problem-solving and decision-making do not end with analysis. Those pieces that you have spread before you must come back together as a meaningful whole if you are to profit by the analysis. This is done through a reflective process of *synthesis*, in which you pull things back together according to your own values. Your ability to make positive changes in your life depends tremendously on how willing you are to devote time to reflection about what makes you feel most alive, what life means to you, and how you can live out that meaning. And all of these things depend on understanding what you value, what is most important to you. If you are unclear about your values, then of course you are unclear about how to synthesize your observations into a meaningful whole.

Take Marcia, for instance. Marcia, a young woman of thirty, has no direction in her life. Never married, she changes men in her life with the season of the year, and she has never held a permanent job. She may tell you one month that she is "dealing in a very big way in gems" only for you to find out from someone else that she is polishing the Indian jewelry that her brother makes; or that she has a "very impressive sales position" only for you to discover that she is selling hairbrushes door to door.

When Marcia analyzes her situation, she tells herself that it is only natural that she can't find her way. The offspring of an unhappy marriage, she has not seen her father since she was six, and her mother died when she was fourteen. Left to live with relatives, she felt alienated and unloved. She synthesizes this as follows: "It's no wonder my life is a mess. Look what they did to me. I never had a chance. Nobody thinks I'm important. But that doesn't bother me!" Then off she goes on another one of her fantasy trips about her next "important venture."

Part of Marcia's problem is that she constantly fails in analyzing what has happened to her and refuses to deal with the *pain* that she has experienced as a result. Analysis of a human problem involves good thinking skills as well as an understanding of your emotions connected to the problem. It is emotional energy that powers any intention to change one's life, and Marcia has deprived herself of these emotions. Constantly in pain, she struggles to deny that pain, and as a result lives with the fear that she is inadequate and unworthy.

Only until Marcia decides what is important to her, and goes after that, will she begin to move forward. And only when she analyzes how she has chosen to deal with the pain she has experienced throughout her life will she be able to take responsibility for the way she deals with that now.

In trying to direct your own life changes, are you analyzing and synthesizing the situation through a clear system of values, and are you thinking through your feelings instead of running away from true reflection?

6. How well do you *hypothesize* about your future course of action? When you say, "If I choose this, then . . ." you are hypothesizing about the consequences of a decision. The trouble with most people's hypothesizing in major personal decisions is that they are rather myopic in their vision of what might result. Good hypothesizing depends greatly on good perception. In major life decisions, most of us will find that at least a few critical consequences result that we have not foreseen. Poor

hypothesizing means setbacks and disappointments and often depression for a time. In your own hypothesizing about the consequences of a decision you might like to make, do you allow your imagination to stretch far enough to envision many possible consequences rather than just those you desire? By anticipating possible consequences, you are better equipped to deal with them if they actually occur.

7. How well do you *verify* your hypotheses? To get a better view of how realistic your "If . . . then . . ." statements are, you must be willing to engage in a certain amount of experimenting and questioning. However, in your own life you will seldom have the luxury of experimenting with personal decisions the way a scientist is able to experiment to test his hypotheses. When, for instance, many young men in the United States fled the country to avoid fighting in the Vietnam War, it was very nearly impossible for them to hypothesize adequately the details of the consequences. They could not verify their hypothesis, "If I dodge the draft, then some day I will be allowed to return to my country under an Amnesty Act"; it was anybody's guess what future policy would be established concerning this painful issue. In such a crucial life decision as this, one must be prepared to hypothesize the most negative consequences and be prepared to pay the price because of the values he or she holds.

On the other hand, it is much easier to "verify" a hypothesis such as, "If I leave corporate life and start my own business, then I can earn as much money and not have the aggravation of corporate politics." Such a hypothesis can be tested by questioning other people who have had the experience; by experimenting with freelance projects; by researching your potential for success in the given market; by questioning your family about their feelings on the decision, and so on. (We put the word "verify" in quotation marks above, you will note, since, wherever the human element is involved, absolute certainty never exists.)

8. How well do you *choose your options?* If you have developed the first seven mental skills in decision-making, you will not find it difficult to choose among the alternatives available to you; for choosing depends on all the processes mentioned above. "Hold it," you may say. "It really isn't as simple as that. When I'm making a decision about my life, it feels as though my mind is going around in circles." Well, that is not an inappropriate feeling, because the decision-making process *is* circular.

When making a decision, we do not proceed rigidly from observation to analysis to hypothesis, etc. These components are related to each other in a circular fashion; that is, our thinking at any one stage could affect our thinking in another stage. Likewise, the mental skills that we use mostly in one component, we also use from time to time in all the other components. For example, when we experiment, we also use our powers of observation. In this circular process, our goals are gradually shaped and, finally, we choose those actions that we think are consistent with our values and that will help us realize our goals. Unfortunately, our negative thoughts and feelings often prevent us from committing ourselves to our goals. We will discuss this aspect of the decision-making process in Chapter Nine.

Chapter Five

Your Dominant Tendencies: The Road Map of Your Mind

As you recognized your own thoughts and feelings in the previous chapters, you probably saw a pattern in them that is affecting your decision-making. Each of us has patterns of thinking and feeling called "dominant tendencies." These dominant tendencies may be positive ones that propel you forward and help you to find a sense of fulfillment in your life, or they may be negative ones that cause you to feel that life somehow never works for you. By coming to understand your dominant tendencies, you can reach a fuller understanding of yourself, and see how you can begin cultivating the tendencies that will give you the courage to change your life into a more fulfilling one.

Just what is a tendency? It is a propensity, or leaning toward, the same way of responding over and over. In experiencing a particular tendency, we habitually behave, think, and feel in certain ways. For example, Midge seems to have a tendency toward alcohol. She has certain definite ideas and feelings concerning how alcohol will relieve her tension and emotional pain, and she behaves in definite ways to get it. We can explain her ideas, feelings, and behaviors in a more basic and comprehensive way by saying that Midge has a tendency toward *dependence*.

You can think of this theory of human tendencies that we are about to describe as a road map of your mind. In reading the previous chapters, you have identified your thoughts, feelings, and actions concerning a decision you are about to make. In this chapter, you will see that those feelings, thoughts and actions combine to form particular human tendencies. Some tendencies lead to self-destruction, some to short-term self-profit, and some to genuine growth. At the end of this chapter, you will have identified the tendencies you have been experiencing most.

The following chart of our tendencies was introduced by one of the authors of this book, J. J. McMahon, in his book *Between You and You.*

The Human Tendencies Profile

IRRATIONAL	RATIONAL	SUPRA-RATIONAL
confusion	order	vision
dependence	control	freedom
rebellion	system	change
doubt	certainty	creativity
↓	↓	↓
leads to self-destruction	leads to self-profit	leads to genuine growth

Although all three types of tendencies are operating to some degree in us at all times, in various situations we function *predominantly* irrationally, rationally, or more-than-rationally.

The following episodes in the lives of three people show how these tendencies are expressed in thoughts and behavior. The first person follows her irrational tendencies, and her decisions are self-defeating; the second lives rationally, and his tendencies lead to self-profit; and the third person lives more-than-rationally, which results in a feeling of growth, creativity, and harmony. After each episode we develop a fuller picture of the tendencies operating in each person to shape his or her decisions. This information will help you to know some of the depth and range of *your* tendencies and thereby see how your patterns are affecting the choices you make about your life.

On the Road to Self-destructive Decisions: Profile of a Person Living IRRATIONALLY

Pam is an attractive, amiable, and intelligent twenty-seven-year-old single woman living with her mother in New York City. Having dropped out of college when she was twenty, she has been working as a secretary for the past seven years, but is now thinking about returning to school to complete a degree. In the following portion of an interview with her counselor, you will see how Pam's irrational tendencies have been dominating her outlook on life.

C: Pam, it seems that going back to school is one of your major concerns.

P: Yes, I want to go back, but I really don't know what to major in. I had the same problem when I was at college eight years ago.

C: What are your major interests?

P: Well, I like fine arts, but I also might like to be a model. My friends tell me I could still have a career in modeling. Then sometimes I think that I'd like to be a buyer for a large department store. My mother said I'd do well at that. My friend, Ginger, is a flight attendant and gave me an application for the airlines, so I'm going to apply for a flight attendant's position, just in case I don't go back to school. Ginger is going to review my answers before I send in the application, because I'm not very good at answering those questions.

C: It seems that you are not clear about what interests you most.

P: No, I'm not. My mother tells me that I should study marketing. But when I was in high school she told me to take a commercial program, and I did. That didn't help me much. You know . . . the funny thing is, I usually end up doing what she suggests.

C: You don't always appreciate her advice, but you take it anyway. How does that make you feel?

P: Oh, I just try to keep the peace. She lectures all the time anyway.

C: How does that make you feel?

P: Well, I wish she would mind her own business about some things.

C: Like?

P: Like my friends. Especially my boyfriends.

C: You would like your mother to keep her opinions to

herself, and yet when she expresses them, they influence your behavior.

P: I guess I trust her judgment more than my own.

C: Pam, it seems that you don't place much confidence in your own thinking.

P: I wish I could trust myself to make up my own mind about what I want to do. I'm always depending on others for the answers. And the answers never work. Look at me. Twenty-seven. And nowhere. I just don't know what to do.

As the interview continued, it became apparent that Pam frequently felt *confused* about important matters in her life. She usually *depended* on the advice of her mother or her friends to guide her thinking. If she failed or was disappointed after taking their advice, Pam would *rebel* against them with a simmering anger. After cooling off, she would indulge herself in morbid *doubt* by mumbling to herself, "Who can you trust anyway?" Unfortunately, Pam functions predominantly according to her *irrational* tendencies. As a result, she does not do her own thinking or make her own decisions. If she continues to live this way, she will eventually see her life as being destroyed by other people. After all, aren't they the ones who got her into this mess by telling her what to do? It's the perfect alibi for the confused, dependent person.

The irrationalities so characteristic of Pam—like most irrational behavior—have their base in Pam's cutting off her deepest feelings from herself. Notice in the dialogue that Pam does not acknowledge the anger she feels toward her mother. Until Pam becomes more in touch with her own feelings, she will not be able to find meaning in those feelings to direct her *own* life.

Let's take a closer look at each irrational tendency to discover which one might be sabotaging *your* decision-making.

CONFUSION

How many times have you caught yourself saying, "I just don't know what to do about my life. I'm really confused. Something's got to come along to change this."

Confusion is a failure to distinguish between things. The confused person often has great difficulty in mentally processing the feelings he or she is experiencing, which causes an inability to make reasonable value judgments.

The following questions will help you pinpoint areas of confusion in your own life as you go about making decisions.

1. Are you unclear about what is most important to you in life?

2. Do you lack purpose in what you do?

3. Do you think or feel one way but behave in another?

4. Are you unclear about how you see yourself?

5. Are you unable to set clear goals and work toward reaching them?

If you answered "yes" to most of these questions, you are operating from the position of confusion in any attempt you make to change. When you feel so unsure about yourself, you are very likely allowing others to make your decisions *for* you.

DEPENDENCE

Irrational dependence is the easiest of all the irrational traps to fall into. Why do we say *irrational* dependence? Because there is a certain degree of dependence in any significant relationship, and it is only when we lose control of our own freedom of choice that it becomes irrational dependence.

The awareness of your own freedom is a fundamental requirement for your emotional well-being; and the moment you begin to turn that freedom over to someone else is the moment that your confusion and dependence begin.

Do you recognize the tendency of dependence in your own decisions about your life? Are you dependent, for instance, on your job title for your sense of identity? Does your feeling of security hinge so tightly on your present job that if you lost it you would be immobile to exercise the freedom of your mind to find another satisfying position? Are you dependent on a friend, parent, spouse, or therapist to make your decisions for you? Do you depend on someone else to bring the happiness into your life? If so, you are experiencing irrational dependence.

How do you respond to the following questions?

1. Do you usually seek someone's approval or advice before acting?

2. Do you feel unsure about your judgments?

3. Do you have the feeling that someone is always evaluating you?

4. Are your ideas about yourself simply a reflection of the way you think people see you?

5. Do you usually choose a very dominant person in a love relationship?

If you answered "yes" to most of these questions, you need to take a close look at what is important to you and to begin taking responsibility for your own life. And that is easier said than done. Throwing off dependence demands tremendous self-reflection and a certain level of courage to confront your fears, insecurities, and anxieties. It means working on yourself, the way you would any special project, to begin building your own self-esteem.

REBELLION

Rebellion is the natural consequence of dependence. If you are dependent in your relationships, you will be able to recall many times that you have felt let down because the person (thing) you depended upon failed you. You then felt angry, right? And wanted to punish the person or thing for not assuming proper responsibility for your life? At that time, any decision you took most likely became one of rebellion: "I'll show him (her, them, it)."

Is your tendency toward rebellion preventing you from making effective decisions about changing your life?

1. Do you expect people to behave according to your needs all the time?

2. When things do not go your way, do you withdraw and sulk?

3. Do you usually blame others for your unhappiness?

4. Do you get to a point in situations that you feel you have to prove your independence?

5. Are most of your major decisions *away from* something (somebody) rather than *toward* something (somebody)?

Affirmative answers to most of these questions indicate that you are letting rebellion control your decisions. And rebellious decisions rarely lead to satisfying consequences.

DOUBT

Anyone who has worked in the corporate environment knows the DESOP game (Defensive Strategies for Office Personnel). The game is played on the principle that all those people out there are basically dishonest. An example of this strategy is to protect yourself by putting everything in writing. If you just had a business conversation with an associate, you have to write a memo to him documenting what you just told him. And don't forget the "copies to . . ." You may master these tactics on the assumption that "they" are out to get you. Indeed, there probably are some people trying to knock you off the corporate ladder. But if you become doubtful of *everyone*, you will fall off all by yourself.

While there are always people in our lives who don't deserve to be trusted, doubting the good intentions of *everyone* is really the result of our own weakness. If we have no confidence in ourselves, we become small in our own eyes, while everyone around us seems like giants. "Why would they be interested in giving *me* a fair shake?" we ask.

If you find that you doubt people in general, you will probably find that in your adult years you have chosen to let other people take responsibility (or the illusion of it) for your life and have been sorely disappointed.

Check your own tendency to doubt others by answering these questions:

1. Do you usually believe the worst about people?

2. Are you afraid to speak openly and honestly to your friends?

3. Is your criticism usually negative, rather than constructive?

4. Do you spend more time thinking about your own deficiencies than about your potential?

5. When people offer to do something for you, do you usually search for their hidden, selfish motives?

If you answered "yes" to most of the twenty questions on these last pages, you are most likely on the road to self-destructive decisions. And regardless of what list of techniques you read to try to stop being the victim, the only lasting way out of this dilemma is through self-reflection and responsible choice.

On the Road to Decisions of Self-profit: Profile of a Person Living RATIONALLY

Bill Maus, who prides himself on being a former military officer, is now the dean of administration at a state university. In his military career he learned the importance of order. Bill was grateful for this experience because it taught him that his success depended on how organized he was.

As dean of administration, Bill is responsible for all the business aspects of the college community—purchasing, payroll, personnel, maintenance, budget control, financial aid, registration, the computer center, etc. Upon assuming his new position, he had each supervisor prepare a detailed report on the goals and procedures of his or her department. Knowing the *order* that should exist in each area of his division, Bill now felt in full *control* of the people under him. After knowing how each operation was supposed to function, he felt more confident about using his authority to make decisions. He also knew that he was in a better position to make changes because he now saw how all the operations of his division were interrelated in one *system*. When he noticed that the whole system was not moving smoothly, he concluded that some departments in his division were not achieving their goals. Bill wanted to be *certain* that all the goals of his division were reached on budget, on time. Consequently, he spent many hours perfecting the procedures and interpersonal communications within and among the departments of his division. Within a few months Bill's division was operating with clockwork precision. Because he believed that the performance of his division would reflect a good or poor image of himself to the rest of the college community, Bill put in long days of tedious analysis and planning. For him, excellent performance by his staff and a good image of himself added up to his own *self-profit*. He felt that all his work was handsomely rewarded when at the end of his second year as dean, he received the Distinguished Administrator's award.

Bill's system of control and order definitely leads to a certain amount of self-profit. After all, he received the Distinguished Administrator's award, didn't he? But what about the fuller picture of Bill's life?

Bill wonders why his life has no real highs; he envies people who have the courage to take risks and adventure out on some new endeavor. He realizes that he takes a safe, controlled approach to life. And as far as his goals for success in his work go, that approach seems to be working. But why does he feel so empty? he wonders.

Why is it that as Bill comes each step closer to his goal, he feels emptier? Why isn't the rational tendency of self-profit enough to make him feel in tune with his life? After all, he's read every self-help book he can find on success and control. He's learned all the techniques. He's getting the results they say he should. So why isn't that enough?

Bill's rational system of self-profit is a good one, but only when combined with the supra-rational tendencies that lead to emotional growth. Without this combination, Bill becomes like many people in our society: groping for success, fighting for control over others, dreaming of how someday his calculated system is going to see him to his goal of money and prestige.

Let's look at the characteristics of the purely rational person and find out why they may lead to self-profit and yet not a feeling of emotional growth.

ORDER

Part of the beauty of the universe is that with all its complexity it has a miraculous order. We, as human beings, are also able to construct the beauty of order in our life if we understand that our *true* order does not derive from patterns and activities that we construct outside ourselves, but instead from those we construct from within ourselves.

For many of us, feelings of confusion or chaos trigger a search for "authorities" who will help us put order back into our life. For example:

If you feel confused and frustrated as a parent, do you look for that "how-to-be-a-great-parent" manual?

If your sex life is in trouble, do you reach for your handy "how-to" sex book?

If your social life is in shambles do you sign up for a course on how to win friends?

If you are dissatisfied with your religious life, do you begin looking for the book that tells you the ten secret and sure ways of reaching God?

The list goes on and on. If you have reflected about your feelings, you have developed your vision of what is fundamentally important to you and can easily see that the realization of your goals is not in following a list of do's and don'ts so readily available. The pattern of actions that helps you to realize your goals as a parent, worker, spouse, or whatever else, grows out of the internal *process* of getting in touch with your deepest thoughts about the meaning of your life. After you have widened your vision of your values and your deepest thoughts about what you value, you will be able to write your own "how-to" manuals. The following questions will help you discover whether the order of your life is authentically yours or is someone else's that you have superimposed on yourself.

1. Do you have enough control of your emotions so that

your activities are not disrupted by extreme mood swings?

2. Are you in the habit of setting goals for your personal and career development?

3. Do you feel organized in your life?

4. Do you usually have a good reason for what you're doing?

5. Do you prudently limit your activities so that you are not spread too thin?

The rational tendency toward order is necessary. However, if your decisions are based on an overdependency on organization, then that order becomes *irrational*. There are times in every person's life when he or she must choose to relinquish a certain degree of order if any change is to take place. Are you so dependent on keeping everything "in place" that you refuse to change your life?

CONTROL

Authentic control over our life comes from being clear about what is most important to us, setting goals to achieve it, and having the knowledge and skills to know *how* to achieve it. The feeling of helplessness that we experience when we feel out of control, on the other hand, comes from the feeling that we just don't know what to do. No matter how much we grit our teeth with determination, our ignorance makes us feel powerless. The essence of real control, then, is knowledge supported by determination.

It is in times of true crisis in our life that our authentic control is tested, for in the daily routine of normal life we may deceive even ourselves about our capacity for control simply because that capacity has never been tested in a crucial way. At those moments we are like the fair-weather sailor who appears to be in command of his sailboat because he knows just enough about his boat to manage it in calm waters. He perches on his sloop with an air of confidence until he is tossed overboard by a sudden squall. Like the sailor, it is when we weather the storms of life that we discover the depth of our self-knowledge and skills for living which are necessary to stay in control.

There are two kinds of control that we experience in our lives: external and internal. When we try to manage the people and events that affect our lives, we are practicing external control. When we are clarifying our personal values and are responding to events and people through our values, we are practicing internal control. If our use of external control is not guided by our internal control, we deceive ourselves into believing that we are in charge of our life when in reality we are letting our sense of well-being and control depend on how other people respond to us or on the circumstances of a single event in our life.

John is an example of this false control. He suffered tremendous confusion in his personal and family life after losing his job during a recession. This economic accident took a terrible toll on John's self-confidence, which affected his relationship with his wife and children. He felt that he was losing control. When John was re-employed in a position similar to his former job, he summed up that episode by saying, "My life was crumbling around me (read: "I was confused") and I couldn't do much about it (read: "I lost control"), but things got back together again (read: "I was back in control") when that job popped up (read: "My life depended on that job")."

Trying to live without a job is tough, but trying to live without personal vision and freedom is even tougher. The control in John's life is external; that is, his feelings about himself, the tone of his relationship with his wife and children, and most of his personal, social, and professional goals depend on his job. Most of his decisions are controlled by this dependency. Obviously, John is not in control of his own life.

The other option open to John, and to all of us, is to focus our attention on what is of value to us in our relationship with our spouse and children, and what is of value to us as a person. In taking this approach, we will discover that our values are determined by the powers of our own thinking and choosing. We don't have to depend on a job to feel value in our lives, even though, without a job, we may feel uncomfortable economically. Furthermore, if we operate from a clear vision of what we value and a strong will to run our own life, we will decide ourselves on the pattern of actions that we will use to achieve what is important to us. We will experience the internal control that gives us the confidence to secure the kind of job and lifestyle that we really want.

Ask yourself the following questions to find out if you are controlling your own life.

1. Do you usually feel even-tempered in stressful circumstances?

2. Under stress, do you usually focus your attention on ways of solving the problem rather than on your negative feelings about the situation?

3. When confronted with a problem, do you focus your attention on your personal goals?

4. Do you feel in charge of yourself in the presence of authority figures?

5. Do you feel at ease about delegating authority?

You are in control of your life when 1) you are clear about what is important to you, and 2) you choose to order your life according to those personal values. Even though you might be clear about your values, you may feel confused in some situations. But the answer to your confusion is not in dependency on others or in the easy answers found in "how-to" books. Rather, your answer is found in deep reflection. Given a chance, your tendency of vision will help you work yourself out of your confusion and establish order in your life.

SYSTEM

If we are functioning rationally, once we have order and control in our lives, we want to keep them there. Accordingly, we develop a system of living that allows us to maintain order and control. If your family is most important to you, then that love becomes the principle by which you organize your life. Your personal and professional concerns will revolve around the center of your life, your family, and you will structure your activities as a parent, spouse, homemaker, engineer, neighbor, etc., accordingly.

Decision-making is much easier if all the major activities of your life are guided by your system of values.

However, not all value systems are helpful in improving the quality of your life. A static system that prevents you from making changes for the better works against you. You can easily become the victim of your own system if you are not willing to deepen your understanding of what you value or even to reorganize your priorities. When we speak about a system we are talking about how the parts of your life are interrelated and how they are affecting each other.

A dynamic system of living, that is, one that allows for change, is essential for human happiness. You develop a dynamic *system* of values by:

1. Regularly reflecting on your values;

2. Being ready to change your system as you develop new insights into the meaning of your life;

3. Remaining open to and accepting the values of those people important to you. (Openness and acceptance do not necessarily mean agreement. You can accept the person although you might disagree with his or her ideas.);

4. Accepting change in the people around you;

5. Maintaining perspective (keeping your mind on all the areas of your life when you are making a decision, so that you consider how an action in one part of your life will affect your whole life);

6. Learning the skills that you need to implement your values; for example, the skills of parenting, the skills of your profession, the skills of relating well to your loved ones.

Check the quality of your *system* by asking yourself the following questions:

1. Do you look at your life as an integrated whole rather than a series of unconnected events?

2. Are you aware of how your thoughts, behavior, and feelings in one area of your life affect the other areas?

3. Do your values operate consistently in all parts of your life?

4. Do you occasionally evaluate your whole system of living to see whether it is healthy and productive, or neurotic and destructive?

5. Are you careful not to undertake too many activities in order not to disrupt the harmony of your schedule?

CERTAINTY

We all like to be sure about the decisions we make, but how certain do we have to be? If you demand 100 percent certitude about the consequences of your actions, you will probably avoid making any decisions. Every choice that you make involves a measure of trust, either in yourself or in someone else. Can you be 100 percent sure about the outcome of your friendships, your romantic relationships, your marriage, your child's future, your career, your investments? No. Human nature is too complex for us to ever be 100 percent certain what another person's, or even our own actions will be. Anyone who has ever gotten a divorce or broken a partnership can give endless stories to illustrate this point.

Isn't what you really want in making a decision a feeling of *confidence* rather than certainty? No one can *give* you confidence. You build it up by thinking logically, then by acting with determination to realize your values. If you will have the courage to act on what is important to you, you will feel confident. Since nine out of ten times the outcome of your decisions depends on yourself, you can see how important self-confidence is in the decision-making process. The most certainty you can have about your life choices is that, after true reflection, you are choosing what is most important to you.

While any rational person will attempt to make decisions that are likely to yield desirable consequences, the need for certainty can be so extreme that it becomes an *irrational* tendency.

To what degree is your need for certainty reflected in your decisions?

1. Do you believe you must be 100 percent sure of success before you act?

2. Do you feel very anxious when you experience significant changes in your life, such as changing your job?

3. Do you regularly require reassurances of loyalty and affection from people close to you?

4. Do you prefer to think of yourself as stable and consistent rather than changing?

5. Do you usually avoid making decisions if the risk of failure is more than minimal?

If you answered "yes" to more than five of these

twenty questions, you are most likely making decisions from your rational tendencies.

Are you on the road to self-profit?

On the Road to Growth: Profile of a Person Living SUPRA-RATIONALLY

When we think of people of vision we usually picture great personalities in art, literature, politics, or religion. Their courage and creativity seem to be beyond our grasp. Yet, even great people tend to think of themselves as ordinary people striving after extraordinary goals. You probably know a person of vision, courage, and creativity who has not received wide recognition. Fred, a former student of one of the authors, is such a person. He was different from the other college students because he was a paraplegic. Sympathy—that was the first feeling that we had toward this young man struggling to get himself into his chair on the first day of class. Then he had to painstakingly fill out his information cards with his crippled fingers. "My God," we thought, "how will he manage to hold a book and turn the pages—let alone do term papers and write examinations?" When he first spoke in his slurred but determined voice, he told the class how much he had looked forward to this philosophy class because he thought the material would be useful to him in his major field, art history. As the weeks passed, Fred shared his vision of what was important to him and how he wanted to contribute whatever he could to improve the lives of other people. He believed that if children were taught to experience artistic beauty, they would discover their own beauty as persons and would carry that vision of themselves throughout their lives. For that reason, Fred chose a career in art education. In spite of his handicap, he felt free to do what he thought was important. The rest of us, healthily functioning people, wondered how this most unlikely candidate for an art-education teacher would ever succeed. Never once did we doubt his confidence or determination. But was his creative power strong enough to find a way to realize his goal? Today, Fred teaches art appreciation to delinquent teen-agers who have learned to see beyond the gnarled body of their teacher and to appreciate his beautiful, courageous, and creative human spirit. Admiration—that is the feeling that Fred earns from people.

When we are in touch with people like Fred we know that living is more than just behaving rationally to have control and order and sure profit. Although we may know conceptually that we are free and creative, we *feel* most free and creative when we are moving toward the achievement of our ideal of being most human. People who have a purpose greater than themselves in life—greater than their own self-profit—are supra-rational. They are persons of vision, who are able to transcend themselves because of that vision.

Let's take a look now at the characteristics of that kind of person.

VISION

There have been times in your life when you experienced a deep and satisfying feeling of yourself. Capture that moment again and relive it. When, where, and perhaps with whom, did you experience that rapturous and awe-filled time of being present to yourself? Was it that quiet moment on the seashore when you understood how you are part of nature? Was it that timeless and breathtaking moment when, consumed by the fires of an autumn sunset flashing its brilliance on the mountain foliage, you were overwhelmed with beauty? Or was it that time of understanding and acceptance by a loved one when you felt energized by someone's loving you fully? Whatever moment it was for you, it was the sort of moment of insight that leads to discovering your own vision of what is ultimately important to you.

There are two sides to vision, passive and active. On the passive side, we feel seized by the beauty or greatness of what we see. On the active side, we begin the process of reflection to deepen our awareness of what we are immediately experiencing.

Vision comes from self-reflection. When we choose to concentrate on what we are experiencing, either within ourselves or outside ourselves, we deepen our understanding of our experience. Vision means seeing things first as they are, then how they *can* be. If your decisions are guided by your supra-rational vision, you are opening more options for yourself.

Are you guided by your vision?

1. Do you reflect from time to time on those specific things that give meaning to your life?

2. Do you examine the way you're thinking, to see that you're using your mind not merely mechanically but creatively and in a way that will help you actualize your potential?

3. Do you wonder about the purpose of your life?

4. Do you think about how you can transcend yourself through the contribution you make to society instead of dwelling on material self-profit?

5. Do you define yourself in terms of what you love?

If so, your decisions are most likely determined by your tendency of vision.

FREEDOM

Freedom, your power to choose, resides in your mind. Marilyn, a client of one of the authors, was suddenly struck by her own freedom during a counseling interview. "Wow!" she said. "I'm amazed at the power of my own mind. I changed my whole life around when I decided to stop depending on drugs. I can feel good about myself on my own if I want to."

Although Marilyn was making choices when she was on drugs, she didn't feel power from her choices. Only after she used her mind to get a clear understanding of herself and her values did she feel authentically powerful. While on drugs she visualized herself as an empty cup waiting to be filled with the experiences of life. She began to change, however, when she pushed herself to think more deeply about the question, "Who am I?" She soon saw that she was a full person, with whom she had never been in touch. She didn't have to spend her life begging for experiences that would fill up her void and make her a person.

The feeling of powerlessness frequently comes from

thinking of yourself as empty—down deep at the core of your life. If you believe that there is a void in you that needs to be filled, then you will always feel weak. You will tell yourself things like, "I need success to fill up my ego," or, "I need attention to make me feel worthwhile." That type of self-propaganda conditions you to act out of your feelings of weakness.

In reality, you are strong beneath all those defenses that you have built up over the years. Concentrate on your deepest thoughts about yourself, and you will see that you are a thinking and choosing being. You are a 100 percent full person. Any person who has the power of reason is a full being. How well we use our powers of thinking and choosing so that we *feel* 100 percent is another story. But you *are* a 100 percent person. You don't have any empty spaces in you that need to be filled. What you *do* have are painful spaces that need to be dealt with so that you can take further steps along the road of freedom.

The following questions will help you discover if you have been nurturing your tendency toward freedom.

1. Do you usually feel open instead of guarded in expressing your emotions?

2. Are you continually trying to expand your understanding of yourself and others, so that, in knowing more, you can do more for yourself and others?

3. Do you change the pattern in your life when that order prevents you from realizing your values?

4. After deep self-reflection, can you honestly say that you find little resentment or rebellion in yourself?

5. Do you feel that you are able to move in any direction that you choose?

CHANGE

Change is the most natural experience of life, and yet we have difficulty in accepting it. If our system of values is based on our vision and freedom, then we are willing to change in ways that we judge to be positive. Readiness to change is an essential for improving our life. The following questions will help you discover how ready you are to make positive changes in your life.

1. Do you accept unexpected situations without getting upset?

2. Do you feel confident and unthreatened by new ideas?

3. Have you changed your point of view on some important issues after you have acquired more knowledge?

4. Is searching for the truth more important to you than being right in your current beliefs?

5. Do you accept change in other people without getting upset?

For more on the readiness to change, see Chapter Ten.

CREATIVITY

When we speak of a "creative" person here, we are not referring to an artistic person. A "creative" person in this context is anyone who is transforming himself to be the most that he can be. We can transform our lives through creativity, but only at a price: In order to become creative, we must trust the power of our own mind and its inherent ability to direct us toward what is good for us.

That means we stop asking ourselves:	*and ask ourselves:*
"What can I get out of life?"	"What can I put into life?"
"What do I need to fill me up?"	"What is most important to me in this situation?"
"How can I protect what I have?"	"How can I make my values real in this situation?"
"How can I get ahead of the others at work before they do me in?"	"How can I work to my fullest potential in order to become the most I can be?"
"How can I be sure that I control this relationship?"	"How can I live fully in this relationship while allowing the other person his or her rights?"

Creative people are creative because the questions that are important to them arise out of their vision, freedom, and change. By following our supra-rational tendencies, we develop the frame of mind that contributes to the creative process. In his book *Synectics*, William Gordon tells us what his research uncovered about the psychological states of creative people.

1. Creative people are first detached from the problem. They move away from the issue a moment so that they can get a comprehensive look at it. If your nose is stuck up against a book, you can't read it. Likewise, if you don't

put some space between yourself and your problem, you don't see all of its parts, and you can't make sense of it.

2. Next, creative people get *involved* in the problem by standing in the shoes of the other person and seeing what he is seeing and feeling what he is feeling.

If you are in touch with your own positive feelings about life, you will feel free to let yourself appreciate other people's point of view.

3. Creative people do not rush to a solution. They can live with uncertainty. Real solutions come from attending patiently and intelligently to whatever process concerns you—the growth of your relationships with your loved ones, the economic pressures of your business, the development of your career. When we are in the process of making a decision we need to be attentive to our own emotional and intellectual processes as well as those of the other people involved.

4. Creative people speculate. They let their minds run freely. Trusting in your own mental power to resolve your concerns is a must if you want to release your creativity. Let your mind think things that appear impossible. Allow yourself to think beyond the common beliefs of society. That's how Copernicus discovered that earth was not stationary, but moved around the sun. You can discover new realities about yourself if you take the chance to think differently about yourself.

5. Finally, creative people realize that the other people involved in their problem are autonomous; that is, they are on their own.

Our right to pursue our goals does not include the right to push people around at will to satisfy an irrational desire for absolute certitude, which really is rooted in an irrational skepticism. If we want to be creative and, in the long run, to achieve a reasonable degree of certainty, we must trust our own vision and respect the rights of others to have a vision different from ours.

The following questions will help you decide whether you are living your life creatively.

1. Do you feel challenged in a positive way by the uncertainties that you experience in your personal relationships or in your work?

2. Can you stay a long time with a problem without becoming frustrated or giving up?

3. Do you prefer to work with complex problems rather than routine ones?

4. Do you feel enthusiastic about trying new ideas in your personal life?

5. Do you give your imagination freedom to come up with new ideas?

If you answered "yes" to most of these last twenty questions, you probably operate often from your supra-rational tendencies.

Are you on the road to decisions of personal growth and harmony?

If you are a bit confused now because you see your decisions as the result of *all* of the above tendencies working together, that is because your mind, in its infinite complexity, *is* often operating from all of these tendencies. You can, however, develop your rational and supra-rational tendencies more fully by reflecting on the previous chapters of this book and by getting in touch with:

1. What is most important to you.

2. Your deepest feelings about what life means to you.

3. Your goals.

4. Your power to choose.

5. Your readiness to change.

6. Your power to transform your life.

An Exercise in Self-dialogue

Identify the issue in your life that concerns you most, for example, your relationship with your spouse, the delinquent behavior of your children, or stagnation in your job. Look at the Human Tendencies Profile, repeated below, and identify the irrational tendency that you experience most often when you think about your concern. Which supra-rational tendency do you want to experience when facing this issue?

IRRATIONAL	RATIONAL	SUPRA-RATIONAL
confusion	order	vision
dependence	control	freedom
rebellion	system	change
doubt	certainty	creativity
↓	↓	↓
leads to self-destruction	leads to self-profit	leads to genuine growth and contribution

Is the pattern of your behavior surrounding this issue

determined more by your dominant irrational tendency than by your supra-rational tendency? To return to your most natural tendency—to grow—you must be willing to move from negative, destructive patterns (which we call irrational), to more positive patterns (the supra-rational).

To clarify your tendencies, write a self-dialogue, then label your thoughts, feelings and actions in the dialogue. The following is an example.

Sue is a twenty-five-year-old woman who is dissatisfied in her relationships with men. First, she writes down her self-dialogue. Then she rereads the dialogue and in the right column she labels the thoughts, feelings and actions underlying her statements.

STATEMENT	LABEL
I wonder what's wrong with me? I'm doing almost everything to please other people.	*feeling confused*
I'm just beginning to wonder about myself. Every time I date a guy I'll do anything . . . I mean *anything* . . . to please him. And it's not just with some dates. I behave the same way with all of them. I'll do almost anything to get their attention.	*seeking approval*
But I can never hold their attention. Maybe that's why none of them dates me regularly. I feel so lonely.	*feeling inadequate and lonely*
God! I would like to have a strong relationship with someone.	*desiring love*
But I just don't know how.	*feeling confused*

No matter how much I try I still feel empty. I feel so frustrated. I want so much to love someone, but it never turns out right for me.

feeling frustrated and disappointed

I wonder what it really means to love someone.

desiring an understanding of love

For me it means to share myself, to try to understand someone, to trust another person . . . just to feel free with someone.

stating a personal definition of love

I wonder how much I understand and trust myself.

doubting myself

I guess my behavior in a relationship is so screwy because I don't feel confident about myself. Maybe I'm caught up in the routine of pleasing everyone to get some assurance that I am really wanted. That's right! I rarely feel good about myself.

understanding that my approval-seeking stems from self-doubt

I'm so busy pleasing everyone that I haven't taken time to discover what I feel is important to me.

desiring to know personal values

I have to start to think about what I really value in a relationship and how to make those values concrete with someone I care for.

desiring to change my pattern of actions in relationships

In this dialogue you can see that Sue is *confused* about what she values in a relationship, *depends* on the approval of a man to feel good about herself, and is *doubtful* about her own worth. On the other hand, she is somewhat in touch with her vision of love which she needs to expand and deepen. In this dialogue she also becomes aware that she needs to clarify her image of herself by getting in touch with what *she* values in a relationship. Once she clarifies her image of herself she can begin to behave more rationally in her relationships with men. Her pattern of actions will be based on what she values about herself and the other person rather than on her irrational dependency for attention.

Chapter Six

Reflections:
What Does Life Mean to You?

When his parents refused what he thought was a reasonable request, six-year-old Michael blurted out, "That really is mean. One day you say I can go play with Billy, and the next day you say no, just because you're in a bad mood. You do that a lot. Just because you're bigger than I am, I have to do what you say." Tears came to his eyes. "BUT IT'S NOT RIGHT!" he shouted as he ran from the room.

Like all children, Michael was beginning to form his own moral theory through reflection about his own experiences. He thought about what happened, and about *why* it happened, as he perceived it. Then he formed a moral judgment through this reflection.

Reflection is an important part of emotional and moral development, for it is only through reflection that we find the deeper understanding of ourselves and our world that

allows us to live productive and harmonious lives.
Through reflection, each person arrives at his own philosophy of life. The words "philosophy" and "philosophers"
intimidate a surprisingly large number of people; and yet,
even as children, we each have our own philosophy. We
are all philosophers—whether we have formal training in
that discipline or not.

Have you ever wondered about who you are and why
you exist? When you ask yourself, "What is my purpose
in life? What am I here for? What is my value as a person? What is important in my relationships with people?"
you are philosophizing. Your answers to these questions
or your inability to answer them set the tone for your in-
teractions with your loved ones, your colleagues, and your
community. They are also the roots of your personal philosophy of life, whose fruit will be your system of values,
which in turn determines your behavior.

Philosophy, then, is of practical importance to you because it determines your actions and your choices.

So You Have No Philosophy?

"I really don't know what my philosophy of life is," you
may say. "I don't have a political philosophy. I don't have
a religious philosophy. No, I'm not a philosopher." Perhaps you have never formalized your reflections about life
in general, politics, or religion adequately to realize that
you *do* have a philosophy and that this philosophy is determining your decisions about your life. As you finish
this chapter, however, we are willing to guarantee two
things: (1) that you will have begun to piece together

your own philosophy, and (2) that if you reflect carefully about your own life and these new insights, you will see that your philosophy has guided the choices you have already made in your life.

One of the major reasons that most of us have never really examined our own philosophy is that our educational system does not prepare us to think critically and creatively when two of our values seem to oppose one another, or to reflect upon our life as part of a larger whole. The study of critical thinking, philosophy and values has generally been left to "specialists" on the university level. Therefore, having little or no training in self-reflection, most of us are unclear about what we value except on a most superficial level, and we tend to say that we know "nothing" about philosophy. Though you may never have studied philosophy, you know more about it than you think you do, as you will see in the following pages.

How Do You Form Your Philosophy?

Building your philosophy of life is like composing a piece of music. Thoughts and feelings that a composer has about life are translated into musical notes. If he or she is disciplined, sensitive, and knowledgeable about music, he or she will see the final results in a full composition that may be shared with others.

And so it is with your own philosophy, which is the musical composition of your life, played out by you in either harmony or discord. In the process, your thoughts and feelings are reflected upon and translated into general ideas about life. If you are disciplined to reflect adequately, you will see the final results in a full composition, "My view of life."

A Philosophical Dialogue

By taking a brief look at some of the more popular formalized philosophies expressed in the following dialogue, you can see more clearly where your own philosophy fits in. As you read the next few pages, notice which of these philosophies are similar to yours and are guiding your decisions about life.

After a delicious Sunday afternoon brunch, Linda and Doug settled back at the dining room table to enjoy a cup of cappuccino with their friends, Sue, Larry, and Bill. As is usually the case in these small social gatherings, the conversation drifted from topic to topic until someone hit on a subject about which everyone seemed to have strong opinions: in this case, the Pope's attitude toward abortion and birth control. Linda and Doug, both Catholics, are married and have two children. Their friends Sue and Larry have been living together for three years. Bill, a close friend of Linda and Doug, is a Catholic priest.

Pragmatist Linda: It looks as though the Pope is not going to make any changes in the Church's position on abortion and birth control.

Idealist Doug: Do you think he should?

Pragmatist Linda: Well, how can you have those large families in today's economy? I'm not against having more children, but it's just not practical.

Existentialist Sue: Well, what's your choice if you get pregnant?

Pragmatist Linda: What choice would I have? If I have an abortion I'm out of the Church, and if I don't have it we probably won't be able to provide the child with everything that we think he needs. The consequences of both decisions seem to be negative.

Idealist Doug: There you go again, always taking a stand depending on the consequences. Some things are just right and some things are just wrong, based on standards higher than man's. If we follow those standards, we don't have any conflict about what is right or wrong.

Existentialist Sue: That approach seems too simple for me, Doug. What is the right thing in the situation that Linda is talking about?

Idealist Doug: Look. There are certain absolutes that we all know. I mean, life is valuable in all situations. You just can't take a life because you might be inconvenienced economically.

Materialist Larry: What about executing murderers? We've been doing that for a long time. The murderer has no practical value for society, so we get rid of him.

Idealist Doug: That's the penalty he has to pay for not living up to moral standards.

Religionist Bill: Larry, capital punishment and abortion are two different situations. In capital punishment, society is taking the life of a criminal to protect itself. Suppose someone attacked you with a gun. Wouldn't you protect yourself even if you had to kill that person?

Materialist Larry: Sure.

Religionist Bill: But abortion is different. Nobody is attacking the mother or the father.

Materialist Larry: Just a minute, Bill. In abortion you're just removing a fetus. We are only talking about a collection of cells. There is an enormous difference between a fetus and a grown person who can think and feel and understand.

Religionist Bill: No, Larry, the fetus is a person. Not like you and me, but it has the power to become like us; so it must be similar to us.

Idealist Doug: I believe that at the moment of conception the fetus has a soul. That's what makes humans different from everything else in the world.

Materialist Larry: Can you prove to me that there is such a thing as a soul?

Idealist Doug: No, but if there's no soul what happens after you die?

Materialist Larry: Nothing happens. It's all over.

Existentialist Sue: I'm not too concerned what happens after I die. I'm more interested about the here and now. I just know my life is valuable. And as long as I take responsibility for my actions—whether I have the right of free choice to have an abortion or raise a child under economic stress.

Pragmatist Linda: Wouldn't you be concerned about the practical consequences of your decision? I mean, suppose you had the child. Right now, you're unemployed and Larry is just beginning a law career. Is this the time you would choose to have a child?

Existentialist Sue: As a responsible person, I would have to think of the consequences, but I think I would want to do what is meaningful to me. Just looking at whether the consequences are convenient or not won't tell me what life means to me.

Idealist Doug: Right. You have to do the meaningful

thing, but we all have ideas about what a good life is. Those ideals tell us what is expected of us in different situations.

Materialist Larry: Doug, where do those ideals come from? I don't think my ideals are the same as yours.

Idealist Doug: It's just common sense, Larry. Everybody knows what a good person is. We all recognize a good person when we see one. I think we're born with these ideals. It's something like being programmed. Inside us we have a program that tells us how to behave as good human beings, but sometimes we break down . . . just like a computer.

Existentialist Sue: Well, no thanks, Doug. I don't want to think of myself as a computer. That's like saying we don't have to take responsibility for our beliefs, our values—we're just programmed with them. What happens to my freedom and spontaneity if all I can do is live out a program? I like the adventure of choice in my life. You know . . . searching out new experiences and ideas and deciding how I want to think about them.

Pragmatist Linda: Yeah . . . but that's risky. I mean, you can easily lose control of the situation and end up being dissatisfied. I like to know that the outcome is going to be a good one.

Materialist Larry: You people make life too complicated. Look, you are born, you die, and that's it. You make the best of what comes in between by using your intelligence to make things work.

Religionist Bill: What do you mean when you say, "make the best of what comes in between"?

Materialist Larry: Make the best world you can . . . like getting rid of poverty, crime, war, and all kinds of injustice.

Idealist Doug: Right. And the only way you can do that is by living up to your ideals.

Materialist Larry: No, Doug. The way you do that is by learning all you can about yourself through science. We have to live according to the laws of science; *then* we will have a good life.

Religionist Bill: You say that science is what's important. But science doesn't tell us where this world came from. If I am going to think scientifically, it seems to me that I have to look for a cause of this world. Isn't that what scientists are always doing . . . looking for reasons why something happens?

Idealist Doug: We all know that God created the world.

Materialist Larry: How do you know that? What I know is what I can see, touch, feel, hear, and smell. And so far I haven't smelled God. As you said earlier, it's just common sense that tells us what life is about. And my common sense tells me that there is no God, no soul, and that abortion is completely okay.

Religionist Bill: My point of view on life is different from yours, Larry, because I believe we can know more than what our senses tell us. There's more to me than matter, but I can't tell you exactly what it is. To me life does not make any sense unless there is a God who speaks to us.

Pragmatist Linda: Well, I believe in God too, Bill; but I wonder about what, practically speaking, that belief means to me.

Idealist Doug: Belief means that you follow the ideals of your religion.

Existentialist Sue: I have belief and ideals that are not based on religion. But in the final analysis, what I would decide about abortion would depend on the situation. Then I would try to act according to what would be most valuable to me at that moment.

Do you recognize some of your own views in this conversation? No one philosophical explanation comprehends life in its fullness. Nor does the sum of all philosophies present us with a complete understanding of life. The human experience is never exhausted, because life itself is boundless. Consequently, if your goal is to develop a philosophy that gives you the final word on the meaning of life, you will be sorely disappointed. You can, though, continually enrich your insight into the meaning of life through frequent reflection.

If you find yourself carrying on an internal dialogue about what is important to you, you are reflecting and philosophizing. Sometimes we are able to carry out this process alone, and other times we need a competent analyst to help us sort out our values and make wiser decisions about the direction of our life.

One of the basic requirements of emotional well-being is the development of your ability to think; and the more thoughtful you become about your behavior and the choices you make, the more you will feel "in tune" with yourself. This feeling of being in tune results from recognizing what you see as important or good in life and making your choices based on that. It means understanding *why* you make the choices you do and being clear about their value to you.

Arriving at our own values is not a matter of picking one philosophical system from the rack of all value systems. Although we can choose values in the same way that we buy clothes—that is, according to our taste—we cannot necessarily conclude that what we have chosen in that way is authentically ours. Yet, we hear people say they have decided to be Existentialists, Materialists, or whatever, as if one puts on a philosophy the way one puts on a coat. Rather, our values grow out of a creative internal dialogue which is nurtured by our own intuitive insights and by the ideas of life that we find in the various cultures of the world.

Take a moment to summarize your viewpoints on some important value-related issues that arise from your own philosophy. The following chart will help you, since it lists the polar points of view on some major human concerns. In some cases your position might fall between the two poles, and in other cases you might find that you are in full agreement with one extreme or the other.

Man is made of
matter only   matter and spirit

Basic human values
change   never change

The source of human value is
God   The evolving human being

A human being is
basically free to deter-   basically determined by his
mine his lifestyle   genes and environment

A human being
can have a true under-   will always be in doubt
standing of who he is   about who he is

A human being
is basically good   is basically evil

A Philosophical Self-dialogue

To help you develop your point of view on the philosophical issues raised in the chart above we will pose some questions about each issue. Take apart the statements that you make to yourself and examine the assumptions and the consequences of what you believe and what you feel on each issue. In this self-dialogue (or you may choose to do it with a friend) you will understand how your beliefs are controlling the way you respond to the challenge of improving your life.

1. Is a human being made of matter only or matter and spirit?

What is your belief on this issue?

Is your belief based on scientific authority, religious authority, and/or your own thinking about your experiences?

How does your belief on this issue affect your thoughts about aging, death and afterlife?

How does your belief on this issue affect your attitude toward other people?

2. Do human values change or do they always remain the same?

Are there human values that you hold that you believe are unchanging?

Why do you believe that values change or do not change?

3. Are human values set by God or by us as we are tested to demonstrate which values are most important to us?

Do you believe that your values are the result of your own thinking about being human, or do you believe that your values are the result of your belief in God?

Are there times when you experience a conflict between what you value in a given situation and the values of society or of your religious beliefs?

4. Is a human being basically free to choose the course of his life or are human beings determined by their genes and environment?

Are you convinced that your way of living today is the result of your free decisions based on what you think is important in life?

Do you believe that you are free but don't feel free?

Do you believe that because your I.Q. has been scored lower than someone else's that you cannot achieve as much as that person?

5. Can a human being understand who he is or will he always be in doubt about who he is?

Do you think you can know yourself at all levels at all times?

Do you believe that our purpose on earth is questionable, but that in order to avoid feeling helpless we must have a purpose that becomes the incentive to be productive and therefore helps us feel in control?

6. Is a human being basically good or basically evil?

Do you believe the uncorrupted orientation of a person is to grow and to fulfill his greatest potential?

Do you believe that man is basically aggressive and

only learns to control that aggression through the mores and laws of society?

Failure to think about your own philosophy of life in this way does not mean that you don't have one; it simply means that you will never know what it is.

Chapter Seven

Values:
The Compass of Your Mind

Glen clasped his hands under his chin, leaned forward to rest his elbows on his knees and repeated the question asked by his friend, Dan. "What do I value?" His voice trailed off as he repeated the question again. "Hell, I don't know. I don't like too many things about my life right now. All those things my mother tried to teach us to value don't seem to be too important to me. I guess values are learned, and I don't seem to be able to live out the ones I learned."

Dan: Want to try an exercise? Okay, close your eyes and be very still for a few moments. Recall a time in your life that you felt something was out of whack, out of tune, with your relationship to the world. Got it? Okay. Now recall a time when you were even younger and you felt troubled, confused. Okay? Now go further, further, further back. Recall the time that you *first* felt out of whack. What's the memory?

Glen: Well, I was lying on a pallet on the floor. I must have been two or three years old. Nobody was around. And then, out of nowhere it seemed, this big dog ran across the floor, just inches from me. Christ, what an ugly bastard. And big. He stood a couple of feet away from me for a few seconds, then ran away.

Dan: Why did you feel out of whack?

Glen: I told you. He was an *ugly* bastard. He scared the hell out of me.

Dan: Was that your feeling of being out of whack?

Glen: No. I felt out of whack because nobody was there to explain to me or protect me or even to care that this monster was skittering around me. He could have bitten me, for God's sake.

Dan: So your feeling out of whack was feeling that nobody cared about you or wanted to protect you?

Glen: Yeah, that's it. It felt all wrong. But I didn't scream or cry or anything. I just lay there, scared to death, feeling all alone.

Dan: What did you want?

Glen: I told you. I wanted someone to care enough about me to be there and explain what happened. Nobody was ever there. Ever. It always made me feel like the world was running—well, like you said—out of whack.

Dan: So it sounds as though even as a child, you valued being loved and cared for, and having someone help you make sense out of frightening experiences that you weren't equipped to handle.

Glen: I guess you're right. I never thought about it that way. I don't think about those things anyway. That's dangerous stuff. Got to stay away from that garbage.

Hey, speaking of garbage, did you hear the one about the sanitation worker who . . .

Dan: Hey, wait a minute. We're talking about love. It looks like that's one of your values, doesn't it?

Glen: Right. So what?

Dan: Where did you learn that?

Glen: Well, I don't know. I was too young then for Mother to have given me one of her lectures. I guess I just *wanted* it without having to learn it.

Dan: So maybe all values aren't learned?

Glen: Right. But how can you have them if they're not learned?

Dan: How about *out of your intuitive attachment to life?*

Glen: What's that mean?

Dan: That whatever makes you feel most alive is what you intuitively value. When do you feel most alive?

Glen: Well, when things are—sort of flowing. When I don't seem in conflict. When I really feel in tune, which isn't often.

Dan: Does being loved and loving make you feel alive?

Glen: Hell, yes. I have lots of energy when I'm in love and being loved. But I'm not too great at relationships. Remember Jennifer? Oh boy, what a . . .

Dan: What is it that causes this energy when you're in love and feel loved?

Glen: Well, it's that magnificent feeling that someone *connects* to you and that you can *trust* her, and you ease up on "the act."

Dan: "You"?

Glen: Okay, not you. *Me.* I get a lot of energy from trusting someone enough not to have to be putting on an act all the time.

Dan: Then maybe you value trust and connecting to someone—communicating deeply?

Glen: Looks like it.

Dan: So you already know three of your values.

Glen: Yeah. But I don't trust too well for long. Remember when we studied Erikson's stages of emotional development in psychology class? Well, I really got shafted in infancy when it came to trust. Neglected the way *I* was, how could I learn to trust?

Dan: I see what you mean. Maybe you'd find it helpful to speak to a counselor or therapist about that.

Glen: What do you mean? I'm not crazy! Get off that stuff! Hey, I've gotta run. Sure was fun. Great game you've got there. See you later, partner.

Run is the word, all right. Glen is caught up in running from his feelings, running from self-awareness, and running from his longing for self-esteem. He is also caught up in the common misconception that seeking counseling signifies that a person is mentally ill. And yet the irony is that the person who does *not* engage in at least *self*-analysis and reflection is apt to become distorted in his vision of the world and himself.

Glen suggests in his talk with Dan that his life doesn't work. When Glen's *car* doesn't work, doesn't he do what he must to get it repaired? And when he has a toothache, doesn't he go to a dentist so that the pain will stop? Why, then, does Glen have such little regard for his own well-being that he refuses to deal with his own *emotional* pain?

While the conversation was ostensibly about Glen's values, one of Glen's comments indicates that another question was in his mind: "Why didn't someone value me enough to take care of me in my childhood?"

Whether Glen realizes it or not, he has made a crucial statement about his self-concept: he does not perceive himself to be a person of value. Moreover, by not reflecting on his thoughts and feelings, he is denying himself the realization that his parents' inability to love him properly does not lessen his own worth. By not examining his thoughts and feelings, Glen can't improve his situation.

Self-esteem is a basic emotional need, and when we do not feel good about ourselves, the choices we make in life scream out to tell us so.

As you think about a decision you would like to make in your own life now, are you aware of how it will be colored by the esteem you hold for your own person? It is impossible for you to make a decision without making value judgments; and clearly the most important value judgment you make is the one about yourself.

Just what are these things called *values* that determine our choices? At this point, there are four questions that we must address:

1. What is a value?
2. Where do my values come from?
3. How do I communicate my values as I make decisions?
4. What is a value judgment?

What Is a Value?

A definition of value is "doing that which we believe is important to us in a given situation." There are three parts of this definition: (1) doing (2) what we believe is important to us (3) in a given situation.

First, "doing" is the *behavior* that reflects the value.

For instance, if integrity is one of your values, you will not involve yourself in deceptive business practices. Your thoughts and behavior will be directed toward producing genuine products and services that meet the needs of the consumer, while providing an honest profit for yourself.

The second part of the definition, "What is important to us," involves reflection. Only when we think about what is important to us do we become aware of our values. Surprisingly few of us, though, are really very clear about what is important to us. For instance, if you ask your family members or friends to list five values they hold, they most likely will have to think quite a while before they form their list.

Keep in mind that material things such as a home or a car must be excluded from this list, since they are value *indicators* rather than values. A young woman named Ann, for instance, told us, "Oh, I know exactly what is most important to me: MONEY." Money, however, is usually a vehicle used to attain a more fundamental value, as Ann began to see when we questioned her further.

"It gives me freedom," she responded. "Having a lot of money today means I don't have to work from nine to five and have a job run my life. It means I can afford to have my own business and create beautiful jewelry without being pressured to market a certain quantity or make designs that I hate. I make only beautiful things that I love, and I don't have to tolerate someone demanding that I make anything other than what I enjoy."

Clearly, what Ann really values is the freedom to create what she loves and the freedom to work when she prefers. Money is merely the vehicle to those values.

We are a society so caught up in materialism that most

of us have come to believe that what we actually value is *things*. And when we finally get those *things*, we wonder why we still don't feel in harmony with ourselves—just as when we learn a list of do's and don'ts about being victimized or about controlling others we wonder why we still don't feel centered. It's because the answer is in a mental process that most of us refuse to deal with: examining our and society's assumptions about what is important to us.

The third part of the definition of a value, "in a given situation," refers to the particular circumstances under which we must act. Life-and-death issues such as abortion, war, and euthanasia are the sharpest illustrations of this point, but values and circumstances also interact in less dramatic situations.

Take a moment to list your own values, and next to each one indicate what actions you perform regularly to realize that value. Also describe the circumstances that present you with conflicts as you try to live out your value. Bill, for example, wrote down:

VALUE	ACTIONS	CONFLICTING CIRCUMSTANCES
Love for my family	Spend time listening to the concerns of my spouse and children.	My career, which I also value, cuts into the time I want to spend with my family.
	Set aside weekends to do things together as a family.	
	Remember birthdays in a special way to celebrate the life of my family members.	

Once you are aware of what you value and the circumstances that present you with a conflict of values, then you will find that by entering into an internal dialogue with yourself, you can resolve your own conflict. (An example of such an internal dialogue is presented under *What Is a Value Judgment*, below.)

Where Do My Values Come From?

Reflect on your list of values. How do you think they became your values? Your immediate reaction might be like Glen's: "I learned my values through socialization." Because of our education, we usually think of values as things or ideas outside ourselves. We might have been taught that marriage, a home in the suburbs, a good job, and pleasant neighbors are appropriate values. However, if we look closely at such "values," we see that they are only value indicators, not values themselves. For instance, a person who speaks about how important his house is to him is very often indicating that what he values is the feeling of security that owning the house gives him. Or if the house is a showpiece, located in the most elegant part of town, he may value the prestige it represents. And so on. If we examine how we learn values, we will see that not all learned values are authentically ours. They might be ours in the sense that we have tacitly accepted them; however, as Dan says, *a value is authentically ours when it comes out of our attachment to life*. We experience this attachment in those moments when we feel most like ourselves, most "in tune" with ourselves.

How Can I Communicate My Values as I Make Decisions?

Communicating your values means more than announcing your beliefs to the world. To communicate means to construct bridges of feeling and understanding between yourself and another person. For instance, Ted tells Pat daily that he loves her. And he tells all their friends how wonderful she is. And yet he has no idea of how to *show* her that he loves her. He is so caught up in his own struggle for power and money that he expects Pat to devote herself completely to his goal. He does not respect her need to develop her own career, and he does not give priority to any schedule that they have set together. Consequently, though Ted swears he loves Pat, he does not communicate it in the most authentic way: in his actions. Pat *hears* him telling her he loves her, but she does not *experience* his loving her. Does he love her? He thinks he does, but Ted's problem is that he has not reflected about what loving someone *means*. He does not know how to make his choices about his life reflect what he *thinks* he values.

Do your actions communicate what you think you value? If not, then your behavior will naturally lead to choices that defy that value.

One way to consider values appropriate to a specific area of your life is to list both the values and the actions you have taken recently that demonstrate that you really *live* these values. Before you do this exercise, it might be helpful to take a look at the situation of a young woman named Cynthia.

Cynthia would like to make some changes in her life. She perceives her problem to be a lack of self-esteem in her relationship with her husband, to whom she has been married for five years. As a teacher, Cynthia feels competent in her work and in general feels that she relates well to other people. However, she has begun to feel strong resentment toward her husband, Charles, because, as she put it, "He makes me feel inadequate. He constantly finds fault with what I do, and often criticizes me in front of others or makes jokes at my expense. Further, he never seems to feel that what I am doing is very significant, and he always expects me to place his priorities above mine. He always *tells* me what we are going to do instead of our coming to a mutual agreement. I tolerate this because I really love him, and I don't want to ruin our marriage; but I am really angry about his treatment of me."

After several counseling sessions, Cynthia's therapist asked her to list some values she was aware of holding that might pertain to this area of her life. Here is her response:

VALUES	BEHAVIOR REFLECTING VALUES
1. *Self-awareness*	1. Began counseling sessions with therapist about my tendency to let Charles dominate me.
2. *Freedom*	2. Same
3. *Self-esteem*	3a. Teach with competence.
	3b. Run my household well.

Her list, you see, was very short. Did Cynthia, then, truly value self-awareness, freedom, and self-esteem? She *thought* she did and *said* she did, but did her behavior demonstrate it? It seems that beginning therapy was at least a start in that direction.

What struck Cynthia's therapist most about her list, though, was how Cynthia seemed to feel that her self-worth depended on being a good wife, housekeeper, and teacher. The following conversation ensued:

Therapist: What does the term "self-esteem" mean to you?

Cynthia: It's how I feel about myself. It's my thoughts about my self-worth.

Therapist: What would you feel about your worth if you could not teach, did not have a home, and were not a wife?

Cynthia: Well, I guess I would feel worthless because being competent in those areas is what makes me feel of value.

Therapist: And what if today you lost your home, your job, and your husband?

Cynthia: Then I don't think I would have anything to live for. All the things that make me feel my life is worth something would be gone.

As you read this, it is so easy to realize that of course Cynthia's value as a human being is not attached to these specific roles as homemaker, wife, and teacher. Perhaps you are thinking that, if Cynthia suddenly lost these roles, it would be normal for her to feel crushed at first, depressed for a while, and saddened for a long time, but that within months she would regain her equilibrium and feel her own worth again in a new relationship and in new endeavors. That is because, since you don't know Cynthia, you are approaching her story with a wonderful sense of objectivity. But what about your own life? What about your own worth? Is your feeling of worth tied to your various roles? Do you see your value as a person attached to your role as a wife, president of a company, chairman of a committee, or star athlete? What would happen to your worth, then, if your spouse left you, you lost your job, you were voted down as chairman, or you became physically impaired? Would your value as a person diminish?

Unfortunately, when they are talking about themselves, most people answer "yes" to these questions. "Of *course* my self-esteem is tied to my role and my achievements. Of *course* my worth depends on who I know, what I do, how much money I have."

Sadly, we have learned these things through our socialization. When is the last time anyone told you that your worth as a human being is inherent? How secure are you that if you were miserably maimed in some way you would still feel your intrinsic value as a person? Most people feel as Cynthia did: if their possessions are taken away, if their present role is snatched from them, they lose their self-esteem instead of seeing their potential to create a new reality.

However, whenever a person says, "I'm a failure," "I'm inadequate," or "My life is of no value," what he is actually telling us has *nothing* to do with his person. He thinks he has made a statement about his worth. In fact, all he has said is that he has constructed a self-image based on the assumptions he has made as a result of how people have treated him in life, from birth until now. A person who thinks of the value, "self-worth" in terms of position or money is someone who has learned that he is "not okay." Unfortunately, that person is practically every one of us.

As Cynthia's therapist continued to question her, Cynthia began to see that, while she *desired* a feeling of worth about her real self—regardless of her role at the moment—she did not *feel* her inherent worth. Through many counseling sessions, Cynthia began to realize that while her relationship with her parents had not given her a feeling of her inherent value, she was nevertheless able to *create* her own feelings of self-worth. Learning to feel that we are special creatures, however, is not an easy process when we have been neglected or treated unlovingly. Cynthia struggled many weeks with her self-concept, and as time went by, she examined her values more closely. She gained new insight into her personality. Self-awareness, freedom, and self-esteem took on new meaning for her. Her list then looked like this.

Area Chosen: What Decision to Make
Concerning Low Self-esteem in My
Relationship with My Husband

VALUE   BEHAVIOR REFLECTING VALUE

1. *Self-awareness*   1a. Enrolled in workshop on examining and improving self-esteem.

                       1b. Began reading Frankl's *Man's Search for Meaning*.

VALUE   BEHAVIOR REFLECTING VALUE

1c. Had talks with a friend and with therapist about my tendency to let Charles dominate me.

1d. Began a journal recording things that make me feel "put down," so that I can see patterns of my destructive thinking.

2. *Freedom*

(*psychological*) 2a. Began observing the way I think about being the victim in life and began reversing my thinking.

(*psychological*) 2b. Explained to Charles how I feel "possessed" rather than loved.

(*psychological*) 2c. Observed how my anger controls me when I feel pushed into something. Have begun taking responsibility for allowing myself to be pushed.

(*financial*) 2d. Began working for a promotion to head of the department so I can have more financial freedom. Had a meeting with my principal to express goals and desire for more responsibility.

(*social*) 2e. Expressed my desire to have more time for my own interests instead of feeling obligated to spend all of my free time with Charles.

3. *Self-esteem*	1. Have begun to tell Charles when he hurts my feelings and point out how I prefer to be treated.
	2. Have begun a notebook of the things I like about myself and characteristics of other people I respect and enjoy being with.
	3. Reading the book, *The Self*.
	4. Listening to cassettes on assertiveness and practicing the suggested exercises.

Cynthia's behavior, then, truly began to *demonstrate* her values. She began *living* her values, and therefore felt more in tune with herself. She began living more what *she* felt rather than merely responding to the way Charles felt.

If you discover after some reflection that you cannot list behaviors that support your values, it is time to consider whether they are true values that you actually hold or merely learned values that you have not genuinely accepted. An understanding of your true values grows out of your reflection on your experiences. As your understanding of your values and experiences changes, your decisions will change. Therefore, the choices you make today may be radically different from ones you might have made a year ago, or the decisions you may make a year from now.

For instance, Cynthia is at a point in her life where she is beginning to be in touch with her values of freedom, self-awareness, and self-esteem. It appears that when she began her relationship with Charles, she was not aware of these values because she had *learned* to value security and dependence instead.

Let's analyze Cynthia's previous statement of her problem:

1. Charles makes me feel inadequate.

2. He finds fault with what I do.

3. He criticizes me in front of others.

4. He makes jokes at my expense.

5. He doesn't think that what I am doing is significant.

6. He expects me to give priority to his activities.

7. He tells me what the direction of our lives will be.

It is apparent that what Cynthia was valuing here was not freedom, self-esteem, and self-awareness, or she would not have allowed the situation to continue for five years. Rather, she seems to have continued the relationship because it conformed with her learned values of dependence and security. But through reflection, Cynthia began to realize that her desire for personal freedom was in conflict with her learned value of dependence. She began to see herself as a value-maker instead of just a value-receiver. Gradually, Cynthia seems to have gotten more in touch with her own feelings and has begun to see herself differently. She has begun to value her own person more highly and she has felt the tension we spoke of earlier of experiencing herself as she *is* and seeing herself as she *might* be.

Her reaction at this point was *confusion.* "I'm losing touch with who I am," she thought, "and with who

Charles is. I'm not sure how I feel, except that I know I'm frustrated and tired of Charles's dominating me."

Through dialogues with herself and a professional counselor, however, Cynthia began to move from *confusion* to *order* in her perception of her problem. She began to see that her relationship with Charles had been one of *dependence,* and now she was feeling resentment and anger that might lead to *rebellion* on her part. Instead of rebellion, however, Cynthia attempted to move toward control over her own life through a system of rational thinking.

Cynthia, then, was moving from irrational thinking and irrational behavior to *rational* thinking and *rational* behavior. She began to see that blaming Charles for her low self-esteem is irrational; as an adult, only she can be responsible for her self-esteem. Though Charles may make jokes at her expense, criticize her in front of others, find fault with what she does, and say things with the intention of making her feel inadequate, how she feels about herself depends only on *her.* Whether she chooses to live with this person with this apparent need to feel superior by denigrating *her* is another question. That is an issue with which Cynthia will have to deal as she moves forward in her rational thinking and her self-awareness. Perhaps with time, Cynthia will even move on to a supra-rational way of behaving and thinking.

At the end of this chapter, you will see that by taking the time to write down your *own* values pertaining to the area about which you would like to make a decision, and your present actions that reflect those values, you can get a better look at what is really meaningful to you. If you discover that your actions are not supporting the values you say you hold, then it is time to re-evaluate your actions and your values.

What Is a Value Judgment?

In a true value judgment we are honestly and accurately applying what we intuitively know through our sense of what makes us feel most alive. To illustrate this point, let's return to the example at the end of the section "What is a value?" where we spoke of the conflict that Bill had in simultaneously loving his family and advancing himself in his career. The particular circumstances that Bill is contending with are: 1) he has outgrown his present job, and he wants to make a move to a position with greater responsibility and challenge; 2) by moving to a more responsible position he knows that he risks having less job security; 3) the amount of time that he will be able to spend with his family will be severely limited, if he decides to prepare himself for a promotion through extra study and more involvement in the company; 4) he realizes that his wife and two teenage children require his caring presence so that they can experience the fullness of family life. The two values that Bill is in touch with are love for his family and freedom to make his work life more creative and responsible.

Bill carried on the following dialogue with himself:

"I really have to move on to a more challenging position with this company. And if I can't land a more responsible job with the company I'll have to explore the job market in other companies. Making a move is a risky business. Although I don't have the freedom I want in my present job to initiate my ideas, I do have security and more time with my family. By moving on, I'm not the only one taking a risk. I'm also risking the financial security of my family. I'll also be spending less time with my kids and my wife. They are already complaining that I don't share much of my time with them."

Up to this point Bill feels that he is caught in a contradiction. Although both values are important to him, he doesn't see how he can apply one without negating the other. If he spends more time at his career he believes that he will be unfaithful to his value of loving his family. And if he chooses to spend more time with his family, he feels that he will be untrue to himself. Bill is doing either/or thinking to make a judgment about where to invest his time—either in his family or in his career. If he continues this kind of thinking, he will eventually make a false judgment, that is, a judgment that is not based on both his values. He might avoid holding onto both values because of the tension that he feels in trying simultaneously to advance himself in his career and to spend time communicating genuinely with his family. He might tell himself that his family is more important than his career and forget about trying for a promotion. Or he might tell his family that his career is first and that they are second. Both of these judgments are false. If both his family and his career are practically as well as conceptually important to Bill, then he will muster the courage to handle the tension that he experiences in living up to both values.

Bill continues his internal dialogue.

"I don't want to prefer my job over my family or my family over my job. I love both. It's like loving my two kids. Because I love Tom it doesn't mean that I don't love Lynn. But it's difficult to be faithful to both my career and my family. If I let go of one in favor of the other, maybe what is really important to me is my own comfort. That's it! Holding on to both values is *difficult,* but I'm going to have the *courage* to do both. I'll prepare myself for a promotion, and I'll share my feelings and thoughts about this conflict with my family."

In this part of his dialogue Bill clearly sees that love for his family and advancement in his career are not mutually exclusive. He also sees that choosing one over the other is really motivated by a hidden desire for comfort. He faces up to the challenge of holding onto both values in spite of the tension that he experiences. This tension becomes for him a creative energy from which he plans a course of action to realize a promotion and to build closer relations with his family.

From the above example we see that true value judgments are made when our intuitive values are the norms guiding our practical judgments.

EXERCISE: WHAT DO YOU VALUE?

If your behavior reflects the following values, you are most likely making satisfying decisions. The definitions given here are very broad ones and are offered simply as a point of departure for you to use in forming your own definitions. You may wish to add other values to this list. How do your actions reflect these values?

1. *Love*—respect, empathy, and valuing of others (which leads to a feeling of togetherness in the human community).

2. *Rationality*—commitment to responsible thinking as a guide.

3. *Self-esteem*—judgment you make of your inherent worth.

4. *Honesty*—commitment and openness to reality.

5. *Integrity*—knowing what you believe in and value, and acting on those beliefs and values. A wholeness of self.

6. *Independence*—reliance upon your own mental power.

7. *Discipline*—behavior directed toward your goals.

8. *Justice*—acting toward others out of your best understanding of what it means to ensure the rights of each individual.

9. *Pride*—satisfaction of achieving your potential.

10. *Productiveness*—transforming thoughts into action in order to contribute goods or services to society.

11. *Self-awareness*—understanding your thoughts, feelings, and actions.

12. *Freedom*—ability to choose what you value.

13. *Responsibility*—recognition that only you are accountable for your thoughts and actions.

14. *Reflection*—thoughtful, searching meditation.

15. *Courage*—strength to overcome fear when you know you must embrace negatives in order to achieve a fuller positivity.

PART THREE

DISCOVERING THE SYSTEM

Chapter Eight

Are You Ready to Change?

You have a challenge before you. You have chosen an area of your life about which you would like to make a decision. You have partially examined how your thoughts and emotions have kept you from deciding until now. You have noted your dominant tendencies in the way you experience life, and you have reflected on your values and the meaning that life holds for you. You have also seen that the way you come to a decision depends on the "filtering system" you use; that is, the values you have that color the decision that you make.

How, then, do you go from the *actual*—where you are now—to the *possible*—where you would like to be?

Ironically enough, many readers at this point will still try to go about making major decisions the way they always have: by impulse; in rebellion against feeling a victim; and in general, in a state of conflict and confusion.

These people may have read these pages, agreed with much of what has been presented, and may even have said, "It's a great idea to get in touch with my thoughts and feelings. It's helpful to understand my values. It's interesting to see the various philosophical viewpoints and to note the dominant tendencies in my own personality." And yet, they go on about their lives as if they had never read a page.

Why, after we have been exposed to books, lectures, workshops, television programs, and other experiences that could influence us to improve our life, do we usually find ourselves right back where we were before this exposure? How can we be so stimulated by something and see its helpfulness at the time, yet refuse to let it affect our daily activities? There are three reasons.

Emotional Readiness

First, one of the essential requirements for significant growth is *readiness* for change. Unless someone has been thrown off balance somehow, he is usually not ready for growth. He may even tell himself:

"I realize that my fears are irrational."

"I realize that there are many risks in staying just where I am now, even though it gives me an illusion of safety."

"I realize that I am being presented with a system that can lead me to clearer decisions if I just let it."

"I realize that I have been mistaken thinking that I must accept life as it is, rather than take responsibility for changing it."

"I realize that I have been allowing circumstances to control me instead of controlling how I experience the circumstances." And yet, he continues on as he always has. Intellectually, he has been impressed; emotionally, he has not been touched. He is just not ready for change.

Moreover, although a person has been thrown off balance enough to feel the pain that causes him to seek relief, he still may not be ready to change in ways that will let him feel real harmony within himself. Sometimes a therapist can move this process along by helping to throw the client further off balance, thus prompting him to examine what is stirring within. Readiness, however, is not something that can be easily manipulated by an outside source. A poignant example of this is an experience that a young woman named Katrina had with her lover, Erik. Erik, a man in his mid-forties, had an insatiable thirst for knowledge and a mind that absorbed information and concepts like a sponge. In fact, Katrina perceived Erik to be much more of a "thinking" person than a "feeling" person. She also found him to be a creative person in the sense that he had a high level of curiosity and could generate new and exciting ideas. He was a pleasure to be with, always stimulating, always an interesting conversationalist.

However, Katrina felt that Erik had cut himself off from his emotions. It was not that he did not feel deeply. But he did not seem to be in touch with his own values or sensitive in his relationships. While Erik said he valued their love, for instance, Katrina did not see him making choices that placed priorities on their relationship. In fact, she felt that he did not cultivate close human relationships in general.

Katrina gave Erik Dr. Carl Rogers' book *On Becoming*

a Person, hoping that it would help him realize how he was out of touch with his values and how he related to people in general. After reading the book, Erik commented that it was an impressive work and that it had caused him to think about some things in a new way. However, the book was not the catalyst for the transformation that Katrina had hoped for.

A year later, Katrina and Erik experienced a dramatic rift in their relationship, and Katrina suggested that they attend an intensive workshop on personal growth to try to resolve their problem. As usual, Erik's outward reaction to the workshop was one of enthusiasm in accumulating, assimilating, and synthesizing information, and being able to relate it to others in an interesting way. Katrina felt tremendous disappointment; again the result was not what she had hoped for.

As weeks went by, however, a very interesting thing happened: Erik seemed to become more sensitive in his interaction with people, and he began rereading *On Becoming a Person* without any prompting from Katrina. He commented that the workshop had codified many things in Rogers' book, and that now he found it an even more exciting work. The book began to take on new meaning for him, and he began to look inward in a way he never had before. Erik showed signs of true inner change.

Katrina suddenly realized that all her previous frustrations in trying to get Erik to reflect on his values and interpersonal relations were caused by the fact that Erik had not been *ready* for change. He had read the book, expounded to others on its interesting concepts, and had changed not a whit. Something, however, in the workshop threw Erik off balance with himself, created some tension within him, and weeks later he started to become more aware of himself and his behavior, motivations, and feelings. He strove to grow from that awareness and therefore to relate with more understanding to others.

Many of us experience the same frustration that Katrina did: we see something in a loved one that we feel needs "correcting"; but our efforts are thwarted at every turn because, even though the person may agree with our assessment, little positive change results. The person simply is not *ready*. He does not feel off balance, unsettled, in pain. Somehow he thinks that his behavior and cut-off feelings work for him. Only when he himself feels a need for change will meaningful change occur. The best we can do in situations like this is to attempt, through our words or actions, to throw the person off balance. To attempt to manipulate a change by complaints or lectures, however, is usually futile. Some behavioral change may occur in the specific situation about which the complaint has been made; but the old behavior will usually occur again in a new situation, no matter how similar. The reason: real change has not taken place *within* the person.

Readiness is essential for change. If you are not ready to change the way you make decisions about your life, reading this book will be nothing but an intellectual exercise.

Courage

The second reason that someone may read this book, agree with the basic concepts, and nevertheless return to his old, perhaps self-destructive habits, is that, while he may feel a disequilibrium, even a painful need for change, he somehow cannot muster up the courage to make significant positive changes. It may seem much easier just to stay where he is.

To examine ourselves, to reach into the depths of our feelings and thoughts, can be painful. It requires a certain courage, and most of us do not have good role models for understanding courage and for learning to reflect on our thoughts, feelings, and values. Unfortunately, in our very materialistic, technological world, most of us do not have a life that is even relatively stress-free, quiet, or uneventful. We do not have the *time* to reflect, we say. Moreover, with social values and institutions virtually vanishing before our eyes, we find ourselves in the challenging predicament of having to reflect on what we value *personally*, since traditional values—in which we could at one time find comfort—seem to be so readily discarded.

If we are to change our life in significant ways, we must have the courage to grapple with the philosophical question of what is meaningful to us. To disengage, to forfeit familiar ground, no matter how negative, is often very painful and always requires courage. The final chapter of this book will deal with those characteristics of courage that we all must cultivate if we are to take the risks inherent in changing our lives.

Creative Openness

A third reason that many of us find change so difficult is that we have not cultivated a creative openness. We have generally been conditioned by our educational institutions to look to an authority figure—the teacher—for information, then to feed this information back on examinations. Most of us have learned very early: don't rock the boat. Don't upset the teacher by asking too many questions, by contradicting or by questioning what he or she says. Don't "buck the system." Remember that this figure determines your "grade." Very quickly our natural spontaneity in discovery is squelched by negative responses to our doubts, our questions, our arguments. For many of us, our traditional education has given us the painful feeling that we must deny our openness to new ideas, lock away our questions, and not anger our authority figures. Over the years, we have learned to stifle our creative openness.

In the family, too, we have traditionally been socialized to deny our creative thinking. An inquisitive child often becomes bothersome to his or her parents. Questioning a rule of the house is "disrespectful," we learn. Wanting to do things in new and different ways is "disturbing" to the rest of the family, we find. We begin to feel that we are pests when we question or challenge our elders.

The fact is that, throughout our life, our creative openness has simply not been rewarded very often. Small wonder, then, that most of us have not cultivated this marvelous faculty which opens us to new experiences, to new ways of looking at things, to positive change.

It is encouraging to know, however, that we are all capable of getting in touch again with that creative openness that is so much a natural part of us. By determining to begin questioning again, by self-examination, and by a willingness to be resilient, we can open ourselves to new ways of looking at ourselves and others. By a willingness to look at possibilities and examine ways to make them realities, we expand our creative openness.

What we are speaking of here is more than an openness to have things act upon us. We are also referring to the ability to create something we desire out of that. We are, moreover, speaking of an openness, a willingness, to act on *other* things in order to create something new and different for ourselves. In this way, we can truly change our lives.

Creative openness means listening to ourselves, becoming more aware of our power to think effectively, to feel deeply, and to will wholeheartedly, tapping our feelings of sadness, pain, and fear just as deeply as we do our feelings of joy, generosity, hope, and courage. From those feelings we can begin to transform ourselves rather than defend ourselves.

The more we exercise our creative openness, the more willing we are to make the decisions that will bring significant, positive change to our lives.

Are You Ready to Change?

EMOTIONAL READINESS:

1. Besides being intellectually aware that some change needs to take place in your life, do you have strong *emotions* propelling you toward change?

2. Do you sense a necessity to examine what you are feeling and move on the rational conclusions you draw concerning those feelings?

COURAGE:

1. Are you willing to search within yourself to discover what is meaningful to you?

2. Are you willing to act on your values despite the risks involved?

CREATIVE OPENNESS:

1. Do you view your own curiosity about new things as a positive aspect?

2. Do you explore possibilities and try to make them realities?

3. Are you willing to listen to your feelings?

If you have answered yes to all of these questions, you are truly ready to change.

Chapter Nine

Options:
Choosing the Best Path

Thus far, we have asked you to concentrate on *thinking* about yourself and the change you would like to make in your life. Now we ask you to concentrate on how you will transform these thoughts into actions.

Gathering Information

Look again at the area about which you would like to decide. List your options for changing the situation. You may already see some very clear options. You may come to recognize more by getting advice from someone whose opinion you trust. Your list may also grow as you find new information from other sources, such as books or people who have experienced a similar situation. Do *not* get stuck on the idea that one or two alternatives are enough. Look at your challenge in as creative a way as possible, brainstorming with as many people as possible. The more information you have, the more options you are able to see. Good decision-makers recognize that, while other persons cannot make their decision for them, outside sources *are* helpful in pointing out alternatives that they may otherwise have overlooked.

Peter Returns

As an example, let's return to the problem of our friend Peter from Chapter One and examine his options in his troubled marriage with Laurie. You will recall that Peter has been married to Laurie for twelve years and has two children. He is tremendously confused about what to do in his relationship with Laurie, which he finds most unsatisfying.

How might he come up with more creative options than (1) to resign himself to the situation as it is, or (2) to get a divorce?

As mentioned before, Peter begins by reading several books on improving relationships, marriage, divorce, values clarification, and interpersonal communication.

From these readings Peter begins to see a number of options to the existing problem. For instance, he becomes aware of workshops that Laurie and he might attend to learn how to improve their relationship. Also, by being introduced to new concepts, Peter begins to examine his thinking patterns and his values. He learns, too, that many people seek professional help in improving a situation. He becomes aware of the worth of objective sources who are not personally involved in his situation.

Peter also begins to seek advice and ideas from friends. By keeping a list of suggestions his friends make, he can reflect on them at leisure. In talking with his friends, Peter realizes that he also has the option of maintaining his relationship with Laurie, unsatisfying for him as it is, and having a relationship with another woman at the same time. By doing this, some of his friends suggest, he can hold his family together and at the same time fulfill his own needs. He adds this to his list of possibilities.

Unfortunately, many of us do not really consider most alternatives that we are aware of because we have already made a secret decision about what we *generally* want to do about a challenge before we even begin our search for alternatives. Since we don't feel confident that our decision will be successful, however, we go through the process anyway, appearing to be open to new ideas but actually biased toward our original idea. Peter, for instance, has already told himself, "I really have to get out of this marriage. I just don't know how to do it, though, without a lot of pain for myself and, maybe, emotional damage for my family. I feel such a *conflict* about whether it's the right thing to do or if I will feel good about myself if I do it. The upheaval will be horrible. There will be terrible arguments, blaming, and hurt. The financial problems that will come out of having to maintain two residences have to be considered. And how will my relationships with our friends change? What will the president of my company think? Oh, the whole thing is just hopeless."

Thus, Peter begins his process of avoidance. He just won't deal with the problem right now. But he remains unhappy. And he becomes *more* unhappy as he realizes that Laurie is not even in touch with his unhappiness.

When he tries to talk to her about it, she avoids the issue. Secretly he holds onto the idea that he must get a divorce. What he is looking for at this moment is people to confirm this opinion and to give him ideas about how to do it least painfully. At this point, he spends significant time with the few friends who support his thinking that he must get a divorce, in order to bolster his opinion that this is the appropriate decision. What is holding him in the marriage is his fear of the risks for himself, for his family, and his and others' image of himself.

As weeks pass, however, and Peter reads on the subject, talks with other friends about his problem, and begins participating in a workshop on personal communication offered in his community, he begins to clarify his values and see alternatives to his unhappy marriage. Now he sees that by working with Laurie toward defining their values and their personal goals, they perhaps can begin to work toward a solution *together*.

He also discovers that they have been communicating poorly; that perhaps he has not expressed honestly and appropriately what he wants, nor has Laurie.

His alternatives, then, begin to include more than (1) divorce or (2) not divorce.

Peter now can list the options he sees thus far as follows:

1. Stay with the situation as it is, resigned to dissatisfaction.

2. Divorce Laurie.

3. Create a new relationship with Laurie through counseling, workshops, self-help programs, values clarification, better communication.

4. Maintain the relationship as it is and take a lover with whom I feel more compatible.

At this point, Peter has decided that the first three options are the most feasible ones. He rejects number 4 because it (having a lover) strongly defies his sense of personal integrity and doesn't meet his need to have a full relationship with someone. He feels certain that he values integrity and love enough not to accept this compromise. He is also aware that as time passes, other options may be added to his list.

Evaluating Options

In deciding which alternative is best for you, evaluate each option in terms of the following questions. Your particular circumstances will determine which questions are most important for you.

1. What is the anticipated loss to myself and to the people important to me if I choose this option?

2. What are the risks involved for myself and the people important to me?

3. What are the predicted gains for myself and the people important to me?

4. Will my own self-image be improved or damaged by the decision?

5. Will I be able to maintain a positive image in the eyes of people whose love, respect, or friendship I value?

Peter, for example, now evaluates each option by making two lists, one of positive outcomes and one of negative outcomes, and weighing them. He rates each result on a scale of 1 to 4, with 1 being "hardly important" and 4 being "most important."

ALTERNATIVE #1: *Stay with situation as it is, resigned to dissatisfaction.*

PROS

		(SCORE FROM LOW OF 1 TO HIGH OF 4)
1. Positive outcomes expected for my Self	1. Financial situation will be easier.	3
	2. Will feel good that Laurie does not feel rejected.	2
	3. Will be able to live with my children.	4
	4. Will maintain my social image intact.	2
	5. Will maintain my proper image of the stable "family man" at the office.	2
	6. Will avoid the emotional upheaval of divorce.	3

2. Positive outcomes expected for my family	1. Laurie will feel good that I love her enough to stay.	2
	2. Laurie will keep her self-image as the successful housewife.	1
	3. Laurie will have someone on whom she can rely.	2
	4. The children will see me every day.	3
	5. The children may feel more secure.	4
3. Agreement with my self-image	1. Will feel that I am holding the family together.	4
	2. Will feel that I am showing my commitment.	3
4. Expected social acceptance	1. Business associates will see me as stable, reliable.	2
	2. Relatives and friends will view me as caring for my family.	1
	TOTAL	38

ALTERNATIVE #1: Stay with situation as it is, resigned to dissatisfaction.

CONS

1. Negative outcomes expected for my Self	1. Will continue to be discontent and feel cheated.	4
	2. Will begin to resent Laurie for not seeing my needs.	3
	3. Will lose enthusiasm about life.	4
	4. Will miss having the love and sharing I need.	4
	5. Will begin to have more fights and perhaps finally end the relationship later.	2
	6. Will begin to perform badly in my work life because I'm not happy at home.	2
	7. Will begin to enjoy the children less because I feel I'm sacrificing to stay in the situation.	2
2. Negative outcomes expected for my family	1. Laurie may begin to have less self-esteem because she will realize I'm not happy with her.	2
	2. Laurie is getting older	

	and will be in a more difficult situation later if I stay now and decide to leave when the children are grown.	2
	3. The children will feel bad when they see me in my bad moods and probably begin to have a poor self-image.	3
	4. The children will see the tension and unhappiness between Laurie and me and be negatively affected.	4
3. Conflict with self-image	1. Will not be happy that I am living a lie.	4
	2. Will see myself as too weak to make a change.	3
4. Anticipated social condemnation	1. Friends I have discussed this with will see me as afraid to make a decision.	2
	TOTAL	41

At this point, Peter realizes that the total scores for the pros and cons are almost the same. Therefore, he takes the highest value scores from the list and examines only these.

POSITIVE CONSEQUENCES	NEGATIVE CONSEQUENCES
1. Able to live with the children.	1. Feel discontented and cheated.
2. Children will feel more secure.	2. Lose enthusiasm about life.
3. Holding the family together.	3. Miss having love and sharing.
	4. Children will be negatively affected by tension in home.
	5. Will not be happy living a lie.

Peter realizes that the positive outcomes of doing *nothing* about the situation all center around the children. However, he notices that on the negative side, number 4 is also concerned with possible negative effects on the children. Therefore, he cancels number 2 on the left side and 4 on the right. Is he then willing to stay in the present situation to be able to live with the children and hold the family together at the risk of the negative feelings of discontent, lack of enthusiasm, of being unloved, and of living a lie?

Peter next takes a look at the values he holds related to this question and the behaviors he exhibits to reflect those values. He decides that what he values most is love, personal growth, and his integrity.

VALUE	BEHAVIOR REFLECTING VALUE

1. Love

1. Nurture my family with consideration by
   a. Giving Laurie as much affection and tenderness as she will accept.
   b. Telling Laurie and the children daily that I love them.
   c. Listening to the children's problems and trying to help solve them.
   d. Helping Laurie with the children as much as possible.

2. Respect family and friends by allowing them the rights to their feelings and the right to express those feelings.

3. Express dissatisfaction when I do not feel I am being loved in the way I need to be.

4. Seek out people who are warm and affectionate.

2. Personal growth

1. Always searching for new insights; reading Carl Rogers' *On Becoming a Person*.

2. Talking with Laurie about her lack of interest in personal growth and trying to understand how she feels.

3. Introducing the children to concepts about freedom and responsibility, individuality, integrity, caring for others, and striving to be all they can be.

4. Set goals for myself and strive to meet them; e.g., want to get more in touch

with my creative self, and attend Creative Growth Workshop.

3. Integrity

1. Attempt to stay in touch with my true feelings so that I don't violate my true self; e.g., pay attention to the fact that I am concerned about what others will say if I leave Laurie and try to stay in touch with what *I* really feel.

2. Mention as often as possible my feelings of unmet needs to Laurie so that I open my full self to her.

3. Stress Laurie's positive points.

4. Have talks with the children about the importance of being true to oneself and honest with others.

5. Make my choices in both business and personal life by reflecting on what I believe in and what I feel is important to me.

After considering his values in respect to the negative and positive outcomes, Peter decides that his important values of love, personal growth, and integrity will be damaged by accepting the negative anticipations, and he decides that accepting Alternative #1 (staying with the situation as it is, resigned to dissatisfaction) is not an acceptable one.

Peter now looks at

ALTERNATIVE #2: *Divorce*

PROS

1. Positive outcomes for my Self

    1. Will be free to choose a partner more compatible.   4

    2. Will be free to find someone who gives me the love and affection I need.   4

    3. Will feel enthusiastic about life again.   4

    4. Will feel relief to be able to be myself instead of trying to please Laurie.   4

    5. Will be more relaxed at work without this conflict.   3

2. Positive outcomes for my family

    1. Laurie will be free to choose a more compatible partner.   4

    2. The children will not see the tension between Laurie and me.   4

    3. The children will have my undivided attention when we are together.   3

3. Agrees with or improves self-image

    1. Will feel more honest than I do now.   4

    2. Will feel that I had the

	strength to make a deci- sion.	4
	3. Will feel good that I was true enough to myself that I chose a life that allows me to be myself.	4
4. Social acceptance	1. Friends with whom I have discussed this issue will see that I am strong enough to make a change.	3

TOTAL   45

ALTERNATIVE #2: *Divorce*

CONS

1. Negative consequences expected for my Self	1. Perhaps be lonely at times.	3
	2. Possibly not find someone I love for a long time.	4
	3. Be less economically se- cure.	3
	4. Miss the children.	4
	5. Miss having Laurie to take care of household chores, clothes, meals, etc.	2
	6. Miss being part of a fam- ily.	3

		7. Miss the luxury of my home.	3
2.	Negative consequences expected for my family	1. Laurie will feel rejected and angry.	3
		2. Laurie will be lonely at times.	3
		3. The children will miss me.	4
		4. The children may feel rejected.	4
3.	Conflict with self-image	1. Perhaps feel that I am not a good father.	3
		2. Feel that I failed in my commitment to Laurie.	3
4.	Expected social condemnation	1. Business associates will see me as a "swinging divorcé."	2
		2. Relatives and some friends will see me as not caring for my family and reject me.	2
		3. May not be accepted in certain clubs because I am not a stable "family man."	1
		4. Some of Laurie's friends will say vicious things about me.	2

TOTAL 49

Again, Peter sees that the scores for the pros and cons are not significantly different—45 to 49. Once again he examines the outcomes with the highest scores.

POSITIVE OUTCOMES

1. Will be free to choose a more compatible partner.

2. Will be free to find someone who gives me the love and affection I need.

3. Will feel enthusiastic about life again.

4. Will feel relief to be able to be myself instead of trying to please Laurie.

5. Laurie will be free to choose a more compatible partner.

6. The children will not see the tension between Laurie and me.

7. Will feel more honest than I do now.

8. Will feel that I had the strength to make a decision.

NEGATIVE OUTCOMES

1. Possibly not find someone I love for a long time.

2. Be less economically secure.

3. Miss the children.

4. The children may feel rejected.

5. The children will miss me.

9. Will feel good that I was
   true enough to myself
   that I chose a life which
   allows me to be myself.

Peter sees that the positive outcomes to which he gave
the highest score (4) far outweigh the negative outcomes,
and that those positive outcomes, in addition, support his
values of love, integrity, and personal growth. However,
he feels that the decision to divorce is too crucial to
choose without considering the last option he has listed,
which is to make a new beginning with Laurie. He puts
the second option with its scores aside for the time being,
and looks at Alternative #3.

ALTERNATIVE #3: Create a new relationship with Laurie through counseling, workshops, self-help programs, values clarification, better communication.

PROS

1. Positive expectations for my Self	1. Will be able to keep my family together.	4
	2. Will be able to live with my children.	4
	3. If successful, will be happy with Laurie.	4
	4. Will feel free to express my true Self without feel-	

		ing that Laurie disapproves.	4

5. Will feel relaxed rather than the tension I now feel. __4__

6. Will have the luxury of my home. __3__

7. Will not have an economic problem. __3__

8. Will receive more love and tenderness from Laurie. __4__

2. Positive outcomes expected for my family

   1. Laurie will grow and will open herself to a new understanding of her potential. __4__

   2. Laurie will have more understanding of my desire for growth and stimulation. __4__

   3. The children will have the positive influence of Laurie's and my growing together. __4__

   4. The children will be nurtured by living in a happy home. __4__

3. Agreement with my self-image

   1. Will see myself as a committed person who has been successful in making my marriage work. __4__

2. Will see myself as a good
   father. _____4_____

4. Social
   acceptance
   expected

1. Relatives will approve of
   the effort and be happy
   that Laurie and I are together. _____2_____

2. Friends will approve and
   be happy that we have
   solved our problems. _____2_____

3. Clubs, organizations, etc.,
   will view us as a dynamic
   couple who have a lot to
   offer. _____1_____

4. Business associates will
   see me as stable, reliable. _____2_____

TOTAL 61

ALTERNATIVE #3: Create a new relationship with Laurie through counseling, workshops, self-help programs, values clarification, better communication.

CONS

1. Negative
   outcomes
   expected
   for my Self

1. If not successful, I will
   have more pain and sadness than if I made the
   decision to leave now. _____3_____

2. Laurie doesn't seem too
   enthusiastic and may become resentful. _____3_____

	3. I may become pessimistic at having to work so hard at a relationship.	3
2. Negative outcomes expected for my family	1. Laurie may prefer to stay as she is now and may feel pushed by me.	3
	2. The workshops may bring up a lot of hidden anger and resentment, and the children will see our tension.	4
3. Conflict with my self-image	1. May dislike myself for not being able to accept Laurie as she is.	2
	2. May feel that I am manipulating Laurie to make changes she doesn't really want to make.	3
4. Expected social condemnation	1. During the process of counseling and workshops friends and relatives may view us as "kooks" who need therapy.	2

TOTAL   23

Unlike Peter's other alternatives, there is an overwhelming difference here between the scores for the positive and negative outcomes—61 positive versus 23 negative. He sees that if he could realize this hope of changing the marriage, it would lead to most of the positive things he envisions for a satisfying relationship, while holding very few negatives.

You will remember that Peter has already rejected Alternative #1: to stay with the situation as it is, deciding that it is too unsatisfying not either to change or to leave, so now his alternatives are to either divorce or to change the relationship.

Even though the positive scores are not much different in Alternatives #2 (45) and #3 (61), Peter sees that the negative outcomes are significantly different (49 and 23). He also feels that there is more to consider than the raw numbers themselves. There is also that "gut feeling" he has that tells him that he loves Laurie enough to work out their lives together, if she is truly willing to invest her effort in the attempt.

Peter's chosen alternative, then, is #3: to start a new relationship with Laurie in which they can both grow in the same direction and have a true sharing of their lives instead of just living under the same roof with no common interests except the children.

As you can see from Peter's experience, alternatives must be weighed from both an intellectual and an emotional standpoint. The clearest way to evaluate your thoughts and feelings about your options is to make your own list, as Peter did. From your evaluation of those options, your goal will emerge. What do you see as the alternatives to your own situation? Which one of these alternatives will you choose as your goal?

Chapter Ten

Goals: Planning Where You Want to Go

Examining Goals

An important goal is often thought of as a destination that, when reached, will bring total happiness and absolute fulfillment. Each of us knows through personal experience that it just doesn't work that way. Rather, goals are only markers guiding the general direction of our life. Both long-range and short-range goals reflect what we are thinking and feeling about ourselves. If our goals reflect a desire for growth and self-awareness, then the direction in which we are headed is one of growth. On the other hand, if we have no goals at all, it is usually an indication that we are not thinking about growth or change. Have you thought about your major goals in life? For what do you intend to strive? What is the direction of your life? Have you set your goals in such a way that someone else is responsible for your success or failure in reaching your objective? For instance, are your goals tied up with what your parents do or don't do for you? What your children do or don't do to make you feel a successful parent? What your husband, wife, or lover becomes or does? It is important to realize that the more your goals depend on the behavior of others, the more you set yourself up for playing "the victim" in life. If you think carefully, you can recall a time when you have done this or when you have observed someone else doing it.

Carla, for instance, was a woman of forty-eight who became very angry because, she said, nobody appreciated her. She had devoted her whole life to her husband and her two sons, but now her sons were independent and out of her control, and her husband had reached a point where he would no longer tolerate her domination over him. Everything was for nothing, she said; she had sacrificed her entire life for ungrateful people.

In fact, by "sacrificing" herself for her family, Carla had also spent her life playing the victim. Whether consciously or unconsciously, she had arranged her life so that she would never be responsible for any of her goals, which were to have her husband very successful in his business and very prominent in the social circle in which they moved, and to have her two sons very successful in business and be praised by all her friends. By living through her husband and sons she had relieved herself of the responsibility of living her own life. This way nothing was ever her fault. Everyone thought of her as a devoted mother and wife who took great pride in her family. When her husband and sons turned out to be not exactly what she expected of them, however, her world crumbled. Everyone else was to blame for her depression, she felt. She had been tremendously disappointed by others.

Carla's situation is not an unusual one, especially for women. Though women are beginning to find more satisfaction in their own identity and their own achievements, traditionally they have built their goals around their families. No small wonder that so many women have ended up angry at the world and wondering why their life seems meaningless. While significant others often are, and should be included, in our goals, it is self-destructive to stake our feelings of self-worth and achievement on the actions of others.

Preparation for Working Toward a Goal

When other people are significant factors in whether or not you reach your goal, it is essential that you include those people in your activities leading to that goal. For instance, Peter, whose situation we discussed earlier in this chapter, at first feels relieved with having chosen a goal. However, when he realizes the difficult moments he must go through in order to *reach* this goal, he goes through days of vacillating between "It'll never work—divorce is the way out. I'm dreaming to think we can ever build a new relationship for ourselves," and, "I *do* love her; I would like to be able to live together in a way that I don't feel she's threatened by my growth and success. How can I accomplish this?" Finally, he has a long talk with Laurie, describing to her how he perceives the situation now, how that makes him feel, and what he would like to see changed by their mutual efforts. Because he doesn't *blame* Laurie by saying "You do . . ." and "You did . . ."

and "You made me . . ." and because he enlists her help in working together to improve the quality of their relationship, Laurie is more inclined to cooperate than had he taken the position of the frustrated victim.

Peter approaches the subject with Laurie by saying that he wants to do some concrete things to stop the dissatisfaction he is feeling. He simply does not want to go on this way. Is Laurie willing to work with him to make some changes?

Laurie responds that she is sorry that he has been unhappy, but that she doesn't feel the situation is all her fault. She does not feel it's fair for Peter to ask her to change to be just the person he needs or wants.

Peter agrees with Laurie, and points out that he realizes that he made major mistakes in the relationship by not dealing with dissatisfactions when he first felt them, and that it is not his intention to blame anyone. What he would like, he explains, is for each of them to make a full commitment to making the relationship work—not only verbally, but in their actions. Laurie is rather annoyed by this remark, for she feels that she *has* been doing all she can to make the relationship work. "After all," she says, "am I not a good homemaker? Don't I take good care of the children? Aren't your meals ready on time? Don't I take good care of your clothes? Don't you like the way I entertain our guests? Am I not sexually responsive to you?"

Peter, feeling rather frustrated, but trying to maintain control over his feelings, explains to Laurie that she does all of those things beautifully, but that it is really their different attitudes about *life* that put a barrier between them. "What is of meaning to you?" he asks. "How do you see yourself in relation to the world? What does marriage mean to you?" Laurie is stumped by these questions. She has simply never thought about it. Peter continues, "I am not trying to change you to be a certain person for me—to just meet my needs—but I must have a relationship with someone who at least responds to what is going on with me. I am not asking you to *be* my happiness, but I at least need someone who can really *share* my happiness, *respond* to my concerns and sadness, and get in touch with what is going on with me. Where do I put the happiness that is within me if you can't appreciate it?"

Laurie feels rather hurt that Peter is drawing a picture of her as an empty vessel. However, when she reflects on it, she realizes that she *does* feel rather empty. She admits that the way she runs her life approaches the mechanical and that she tries to avoid upsetting situations. She also realizes that she doesn't think "deep" or "serious" thoughts too often, because they, too, are disturbing.

The conversation has thrown Laurie off balance. Peter is not letting her run away from a "serious" conversation as he always has before. Suddenly many of Laurie's blocked feelings are coming to the surface. She feels both relieved and a little angry. She also feels quite confused by Peter's questions of what she thinks about life, what a husband means to her, and who she is in the world. But what to do with all this emotion and confusion?

Peter suggests that they go together to a therapist or marriage counselor to work out some of these things with an objective, skilled professional. After several days of resistance, Laurie agrees.

Had Peter and Laurie built tremendous resentment for one another by this stage in their relationship—and had they been at the point of constantly reminding each other of such things as, "How can you forget that five years ago you left me waiting in that restaurant for two hours and forgot all about me? You never loved me. You only thought of yourself. And what about the time you drank too much and embarrassed me? Or that flirtation you carried on behind my back?"—then most likely it would be extremely difficult for them to make a new beginning. When your dominant thoughts about your relationship with someone are recollections of the particularly painful parts for you, and when you forget the major elements that fill out the picture, you experience a great deal of resentment of your partner.

Fortunately, that resentment is minor in the relationship between Peter and Laurie, however, and that fact allows them to work from the here and now rather than blaming each other for the past.

Another significant consideration in their willingness to work at the relationship is that neither of them has another romantic involvement. Had a serious affair been in the picture for either of them, each step would take on a different color and different dimensions.

Choosing Behavior to Accomplish Your Goal

In listing our goals, it is important to include, as we did with values, what actions we are taking to reach them. Peter, for instance, in his goal of improving his relationship with Laurie, now lists the activities he would like to perform in order to reach his goal.

GOAL	ACTIVITIES
To begin a new relationship with Laurie.	1. Begin marriage counseling to discuss dissatisfactions, expectations, goals, and values of each partner.
	2. Enroll in values-clarification workshop to better understand what each of us values, and set more goals based on our values.
	3. Enroll in assertiveness-training workshop to learn more about positive communication with one another.
	4. Select books to read and share together on personal growth, communication, and sharing relationships.
	5. Share openly what we are feeling.

At this point, Peter is beginning to outline *how* he will reach his goal.

Goals are important because they help us feel a sense of movement in our life; if we have no goals, it is difficult to notice our own progress. Goals also give us direction. When we have goals, we usually know which way to move to reach that goal. How often have you felt a new sense of purpose when you've set out to reach a goal?

Movement, direction, and purpose, moreover, are only three of the positive influences that we get from striving for goals. Many people even find that working toward goals brings a new order into their life as they begin to weave their life into a clear pattern in order to achieve their objectives. However, we do not feel this movement and order unless we understand how to go about reaching our goal. This is done by setting *behavioral objectives*, that is, specific actions that let us know whether we are advancing toward our goal, and unless we understand what actions will lead to the consequences we desire. In Chapter Eleven, we will look more closely at behavioral objectives and how they help us to achieve our goals.

Without specific, conscious goals, making a major decision is a near impossibility. People without goals usually find themselves avoiding decisions for as long as possible, because they haven't even considered where they're going, much less how to get there.

You may remember when your major goal in life was to feel success in your work and be well accepted in your community. Today, however, you may have achieved this goal. If so, it's time to start the game all over: new goals, new purpose, new movement, new direction, new order, new decisions! Life is always there to test our determination to decide.

EXERCISE

1. What are your goals?

2. What is your plan of activity for reaching that goal?

3. Make a list of your goal(s) and your objectives to reach your goal(s). Keep this list in an accessible place so that you can refer to it daily.

Chapter Eleven

Implementing the Plan: You're on Your Way!

Setting Behavioral Objectives

Choosing definite actions that will help you to achieve the goal you have set is a very important part of the decision-making process. To "decide" on an option, and then do nothing to actualize it does not constitute a true decision: unless you make your decision a reality, it is merely thought. Behavioral objectives, like goals, help you measure to what degree you are living your values.

The following are guidelines for constructing your own behavioral objectives:

1. *Reflect* on your goals and values to be sure that you will realize your values in the achievement of your goals.

2. *Assess* your abilities and deficiencies in relation to the goal that you want to achieve.

3. *Define* in particular the obstacles that get in your way of achieving your goal.

4. *List* possible behavior that will get you past your obstacles.

5. *Examine* the consequences of each action on your list. *Choose* the actions that you think will be most helpful in achieving your goal, and state when you plan to accomplish them.

6. *Monitor* your actions on a daily basis and *assess* your performance weekly to see if you are completing your behavioral objectives, which are the actions you choose from your list in point 4, above.

Peter, for instance, begins to work with Laurie in setting behavioral objectives to achieve their goal of making their marriage work. He realizes that if only *he* sets the objectives, it diminishes Laurie's commitment; therefore, he encourages her to be highly involved in the plan. Together they come up with the following program:

OBJECTIVE	WHEN TO BE ACCOMPLISHED
1. Begin marriage counseling to discuss dissatisfactions, expectations, goals, and values of each partner.	1. Next week through whatever period we find it useful.
2. Enroll in values-clarification workshop to better	2. One-week workshop on Peter's vacation period.

understand what each of
us values, and set more
goals from our values.

3. Enroll in assertiveness-   3. Next month, two nights
   training workshop to   per week for the month.
   learn more about posi-
   tive communication with
   one another.

4. Select books to read   4. Saturday
   together on personal
   growth, communication,
   and sharing relation-
   ships.

5. Share openly what we   5. Always
   are feeling.

Had Peter constructed and tried to implement this plan alone, it would have been doomed to failure because Laurie would have felt that it was Peter's show for him to play out alone. While she may have participated in some of the activities, it is doubtful that she would have made a full commitment to the transformation of the relationship because she would not have had the opportunity to participate in the planning of that transformation.

In planning how to carry out a decision by setting behavioral objectives, then, it is essential to include others who will be involved in the success or failure of the venture. If you fail to include appropriate others in the decision-making process, you will probably find that those people will feel manipulated, alienated, and resentful of being expected to help fulfill objectives they have not participated in setting.

Objectives set, Peter and Laurie now spend several months in pursuit of a more fulfilling relationship. Elated at first by Laurie's cooperation, Peter experiences a setback when Laurie, in the assertiveness-training workshop, begins to get in touch with quite a bit of anger she has been hiding in her passivity for so many years. "I've created a monster; I made the wrong decision. Why didn't we just get a divorce?" he begins to think, and goes through a period of friction with Laurie far exceeding any they have ever known before.

At this point, he becomes rather depressed that he chose the alternative he did, and thinks of reversing the decision by getting a divorce. He simply had not anticipated anger from Laurie of a strength and depth he had never seen in her before. Through their marriage-counseling sessions and with the assistance of the facilitator of their assertiveness workshop, however, they work through this period.

The marriage counselor explains to them both that Laurie's reaction is quite normal for a person who has taken a passive position for so long. By getting in touch with so many of her repressed thoughts and feelings all at once, Laurie is reacting much more strongly than had she been acknowledging them as they occurred. Her strong emotions, the counselor points out, are directed as much at herself as at Peter, and most likely she will begin to feel more comfortable with herself in a matter of weeks or months.

As time passes, Peter is pleased to find that Laurie has become a far more interesting woman than before, in touch with many new feelings, more assertive, more self-confident. His fears that he made a drastic error subside. Their new relationship is truly beginning.

Laurie begins to discover many hitherto unexplored areas of her personality and finds that she now can better understand why Peter has not been happy to have a nine-to-five job, come home and watch television, and, in general, live a basically uneventful, uncreative life. She begins to recognize her own creativity, and enjoys participating more in outside activities. She begins to appreciate how much of her creative self lies in her unconscious, and she begins keeping a log of her dreams. She takes a course in dream analysis, and does extensive reading on the subject. She is amazed at how fascinating her own mind is and how much potential lies within her. As she begins to be more caring of herself, she becomes more caring of others.

Peter, for his part, begins to understand that Laurie will never view life exactly as he does, but he begins to accept Laurie more for herself. He is particularly happy that she has become more expressive of her love both for him and the children. He is delighted, too, that she has become a more stimulating person, full of experiences and thoughts to share.

After several months, Laurie and Peter make a mutual decision to end their marriage counseling and to continue their exploration through reading together and attending workshops from time to time.

Peter is happy with his decision, and he knows that, whereas there will still be difficult periods in their marriage, by understanding their values, goals, and direction, he and Laurie will be able to make decisions consistent with what they perceive to be the meaning of their lives.

Regretting Your Decision

Few people have the good fortune of making a major decision about their life without afterwards experiencing a period of worry that they may have made a mistake. Despite all the rational processes that bring us to a decision, we somehow usually go through at least moments of feeling that the outcome of the decision is less attractive than what we might have experienced with the rejected alternatives.

Not surprisingly, this period usually occurs when there are setbacks resulting from the decision. Some of us experience self-contempt during this time; others take comfort in blaming other people for their troubles. How we choose to deal with this regret depends on our concepts of self and of life. If we have an emotional investment in believing that someone else is responsible for this unhappy period, we will simply blame others for the outcome. If, however, we train ourselves in rational and supra-rational thinking, then we take responsibility for our actions and begin to think creatively about how we can make the best of the circumstances as they are, or we make decisions to transform the situation into a happier one.

If we have deluded ourselves into believing that our life will be perfect if we just make this one right decision, then of course we will be tremendously disappointed with the actual results. The goal of any decision should be to make our life function more effectively, rather than to assure perfect happiness.

What about such regret that lasts for longer than a few hours, days, or weeks? Careful reflection is needed at this point to discover just what is most dissatisfying about the decision, how it conflicts with your values and goals, and why the price of your choice seems too high. It is then time to go back to Chapter One and look at the "what," "why," "who," "when," "where," and "how" questions regarding the area of tension. If you are engaging in irrational, self-destructive thinking, then of course *any* decision is going to yield the same result: you will berate yourself or others because everything is not perfect.

Again, our understanding of our values and goals determines how we experience moments of regret for the decision we have made. We may be sorry about certain outcomes; we may feel bad for people around us; however, if our decision is based on rational and supra-rational thinking about our values and goals, then the decision will ultimately be a positive one. By being clear about what is of most value to us and what we most want to strive for, we are better able to withstand the problems that develop out of the decision.

The persons who will experience the least regret after a decision will be those who have spent a significant length of time considering the negative and positive consequences *before* they make a decision. If they have done this carefully, they have few surprises at the outcome of their decision and therefore do not experience many emotional setbacks. However, if they have not made their decision with a view of the consequences, they may have made a truly bad decision for themselves. If so, they will attempt to reverse the decision if possible, or begin a new decision-making process to try to rectify the situation. It is our hope that you, the reader of this book, will feel confident that your decision will help you function most effectively and fully.

Supporting the Decision

In the period following a decision, it is far healthier to seek out people and situations that support your decision instead of people who are angry with you because of it or who ostracize you for a decision you believe to be consistent with your values.

You must keep in mind, however, that sometimes even during the process of deciding you may strive to support a bias you have toward one of the alternatives, steadfastly favoring one opinion even before you look carefully at the pros and cons of the various alternatives. In Peter's case, for example, he at first was biased toward a divorce, and supported his opinion by associating with people who agreed with him. As time passed, however, he began to be influenced by other people and sources of information that changed his thinking. He did not, in other words, surround himself with people favoring his opinion to the exclusion of differing opinions. If he had, his decision might well have been less satisfactory than it ultimately was.

Being aware of the influence of those around us on our decision will help us to avoid extremes. Occasionally, we might get carried away in our effort to affirm our decision. Some of us may find that we so desperately need to be told that we made the correct decision that we go to extremes to convince ourselves and others that we are "right." This is especially so when people close to us have been hurt by the decision. However, when we are clear that our choices are based on our values and our perception of the meaning that life holds for us, we do not feel a strong need to convince ourselves that we have made a "good" decision any more than we feel tremendous regret about the decision.

Is There a "Right" Decision?

Peter and Laurie's course of action, as we pointed out earlier, is not a "right" decision for every situation. Nor would it be a good decision for everyone attempting to solve the problems of a bad marriage. But it is a good one for Peter and Laurie because *it worked* for them; as a result of it, they became more aware of the needs of one another and began to enjoy life more. Through their workshops, reading, and counseling, they began to feel a *congruency* between what they were feeling and what they were doing. The decision "felt" good. How often have you made a decision and then felt tense, out of place, or guilty about it? The decision, in other words, just did not "feel" good. Had your irrational thinking been controlling the decision-making process, most likely *no* decision would have felt good. *You* in general, in *life*, would not have felt good. When irrational thinking is running our lives, we simply do not feel congruent. To feel good about a decision, then, we must make certain that the thinking which has led to that decision is rational or supra-rational, in other words, healthy thinking. We use "healthy" here to mean the converse of self-defeating. Healthy thinking affirms your basic worth as an individual and propels you to constructive action in your life. It is thinking that makes your life work for you rather than debilitating or destroying you.

Are there "right" decisions, then? Only in the sense that they help us to function more effectively in life and direct us toward the actualization of our values, through which we experience personal integrity. If we choose to pigeon-hole decisions into "right" and "wrong" boxes and refuse ever to modify a decision with changing circumstances, we are more concerned with appearing "right" than with the direction of our lives.

Each of us has observed someone—even one's self—trying to be "right" in a decision: the executive, for instance, who spends significant time in meetings rationalizing to his superiors, colleagues, and subordinates how he was "right." Nobody, of course, is interested in his righteousness. What they are interested in is whether his decision *works* within a given value structure. Does he get the desired results and pay an affordable price?

We have also seen the person, whom we'll call Jack, who becomes outraged at a colleague and vows never to speak to him again. For a time, Jack may be happy with the decision. As weeks, months, or years move along, however, the situation changes and it becomes awkward, even ludicrous, for him not to speak to his associate anymore. Jack even begins to feel differently about his associate and *wants* to speak to him. But he prefers to be "right." After all, he made a vow in front of several people never to speak to this jerk again. How can he reverse such a decision now? "People will think I'm weak," he tells himself. "If I speak to him it shows that I don't stick to my decisions." In the meantime, however, Jack is feeling very uncomfortable with the decision. The associate buys a house on the same street, joins the same club, and attends the same church. Jack hangs onto his emotional investment in being right, however, and begins to find himself in innumerable awkward circumstances. He is unhappy with his decision at this point because it is not *working* for him. He would like to reverse the decision. Only at the moment that Jack begins to think rationally about the situation and sees that it is self-defeating to persist in this game will he begin to feel a need to renew the acquaintance.

A *decision* does not imply finality. It is never "right" for every situation. And it is only as good as it makes you feel.

Chapter Twelve

Choosing a Life of Harmony

Choosing a life that is satisfying and that allows you to feel harmony both within yourself and with the world is not an easy task. It always requires courage; and it usually involves a struggle.

What do we mean by feeling harmony within yourself and with the world? The following checklist will give you some indication of the degree of harmony or discord you presently feel in your life.

1. Do you wake up many mornings feeling lethargic and unenthusiastic about the day ahead?

2. If you had your wish, would you live with a person other than the one you're living with now?

3. Do you stay in unsatisfying situations for long pe-

riods, feeling unable to control the direction of your life?

4. Do you make choices that always seem to make you feel guilty?

5. Do you find that you don't trust your own intuition and feelings?

6. Do you usually feel determined to be superior or "right"?

7. Do you usually feel inferior or apologetic?

8. Do you feel a need to perform, or put on a show to impress others?

9. Do you withdraw into the woodwork and allow others to take the responsibility for the occasion?

10. Do you feel that you should achieve a constant state of happiness?

11. Do you think it is impossible for you ever to be happy?

12. Do you think that you should not have to tolerate much change in your life?

13. Do you find that you are often criticizing others and are not interested in their right to their point of view?

14. Do you find that you expect others to always agree with your position?

15. Do you feel confused about what life means to you?

If you answered "yes" to any of these questions, you are not experiencing full harmony within yourself. When you begin to feel harmony within yourself, you will feel a congruency between your actions and your values. You will wake up most mornings satisfied that you exercise your power to choose the direction of your life and that you take full responsibility for where you are. It means that you choose to be with people who nurture your growth; and that when people inhibit your growth and well-being you have the courage to deal with the problem.

When you feel in harmony with yourself, you will also make choices that allow you to feel good about yourself, to feel at peace. You will know what you value, and you will protect your values in a way that will give you few reasons to feel guilty. You will also have examined your thoughts and feelings responsibly, so that you will have a high degree of self-awareness and you will trust your own intuition and your own feelings. You will not look to others for approval in order to feel that your choices are good for you. Neither will you feel that you must always assert your superiority or righteousness, nor, conversely will you feel inferior and inadequate. Instead, you will recognize your own worth and the worth of others and assert yourself in a caring way. You will not feel that your social face must be plastered on before you go out into the world, but that your true self is quite adequate.

Feeling in harmony with yourself, you will not merely play out your role, but truly *live* life. You will let your act down.

To be in harmony with yourself also means that you will know that you will have happy moments and sad moments; moments of gain, and moments of loss; moments of love, and moments of rejection. It means that you will not expect to find constant happiness. Nor does it mean that you will expect others to bring the happiness into your life. Instead, you will recognize that you alone are responsible for your attitudes, including happiness, and that while others may contribute to that, they cannot take responsibility for it.

Harmony within yourself also means that you feel confident enough about yourself that you do not have to conform to the intellectual, social, or moral fashions of the times. Trusting your own standards, you simply live your choices rather than apologetically defending them.

To feel harmony also means that you listen carefully to yourself and to others. You begin to be sensitive enough to your own emotions that you can empathize with those of others. It means that you respect your own rights and the rights of others, including their right to have a viewpoint different from yours.

Finally, you will feel harmony most completely within yourself when you understand what you value and what the meaning of life is for you, so that you can live with purpose.

Harmony in your life is not an easy thing to find. But the more harmonious your life, the easier it will be to make decisions that will make your life more satisfying. Changing our life to grow and to feel more in tune with ourself is something that we all would like to have the courage to do. Growth is a primary characteristic of all living things. And, ironic as it seems, to grow we must always be returning to our roots about what we truly and deeply believe about being a person. It is as Paul Tillich paraphrased Nietzsche's idea of Self: "The Self has itself, but at the same time it tries to reach itself."

It is in that true Self—the very center of our being, that we partially discover when we unravel all the distortions, all the mistaken thinking, all the unnecessary defenses— that we discover how to create harmony in our life.

Chapter Thirteen

The Courage
to Change Your Life

We have a firm belief that we can recognize a courageous person on first meeting. Recently a close friend introduced one of the authors of this book to a young man who was interested in joining her in a business venture. After meeting with the man for an hour, she said to her friend, "I don't want to be partners with this man. He has no courage." Her friend was stunned. "How can you make such a statement after talking with him for only an hour? Don't you think that's rather unfair to judge someone so quickly?" No, she said, but just to satisfy her friend she agreed to check her impressions by contacting references he had given and asking specific questions that would indicate his spirit of courage. The responses were as she expected. She then explained to her friend what she perceives as courage.

Courage Defined

Courage is an elusive word; it can be defined in part, however, as the interior force of bravery or daring in facing danger, difficulty, pain, or fear. *It is the strength to overcome fear when we know we must embrace negatives in order to achieve a fuller positivity.*

If courage is an interior force of bravery and daring, is it then an attitude? A matter of insight? Of knowledge? Of will power? Of fate? Therein lies one of the problems of truly understanding courage. An undisputed source of courage has eluded the greatest minds of all time.

Characteristics of Courage

Although we may never have a really adequate definition of courage, or understand the definite source of it, there are certain characteristics that seem to be consistent in people who act with a spirit of daring about their lives; these were the very characteristics that the author did not perceive in the young man who wanted to join her in business.

As you look toward decisions you would like to make to change your life, check the strength of your own courage to act on your decisions.

CONVICTIONS

First, a person who has the courage to choose freely is a person of conviction: he holds values and beliefs to which he is committed. As a result of those values and beliefs, he has an inner aim around which he makes his decisions. Notice people you have known in your own life who can never quite decide, who never dare to take a stand and say "I vote yea or nay," but always insist on staying on the fence until all the other votes are tallied and they can rush to the side of victory. These people are without conviction; anything goes as long as it wears the mask of safety. If it appears that they never have a firm opinion about vital issues, it is probably because they *don't;* so ungrounded in their values or ideas, even *they* probably don't know what they think. So they wait, hoping that others will assume the responsibility of deciding for them, and then of course if there are setbacks, later on, they have the luxury of saying, "But *you* made the decision!"

A person with convictions will not necessarily make courageous decisions all the time; but a person with no convictions will rarely, if ever, make courageous decisions to change his life.

SELF-CONFIDENCE

Second, a person who has the courage to choose is a person of reasonable self-confidence, which comes from his knowledge that he is truly a person of value. The genuinely self-confident person, as we have pointed out in earlier chapters, does not rely on his job title for his identity, on his bank account for his sense of value, or on others to affirm his worth. He has the courage to decide about his life because he believes that he has the ability to overcome the obstacles facing him and move ahead to something better. The self-confident person expresses his courage not because he has no fear, but in *spite* of his fear. He acts on his courage, not because he faces no obstacles, but in *spite* of the obstacles. The self-confident person is determined to become the most that he believes he can be. He is confident that the potential lies within him.

Just as it is impossible for a person without convictions to make consistently courageous decisions, so it is impossible for a person without self-confidence to make them. Without a strong belief in yourself, you are further and further estranged from this interior force known as courage.

MOTIVATION

Third, a person who chooses to take risks to improve his life is a person motivated to strive for a goal; acting on his convictions, he has a *reason* to be courageous. But the issue of motivation becomes more complex when we consider the many motivations acting on a person simultaneously. For instance, Gloria, aged twenty-nine, is motivated to leave her elderly mother and move into her own apartment. She holds the firm conviction that each person has a right and a need to develop independently of his or her parents when he or she feels ready to. Gloria has felt ready to for eight years; but she is motivated to *stay* by feelings of guilt each time her mother says, "What am I going to do without you? How will I live? I'll be so lonely, Gloria. Your poor old mother all alone. I don't know how you can be so cruel to the person who brought you into the world." (Her mother fails to mention that she has a live-in housekeeper and a younger sister who lives a block away.)

Gloria is also motivated to stay by the comfort of her mother's beautiful home, as opposed to the Spartan life she will have to live as she begins to furnish her own apartment.

Most likely Gloria will stay, unhappy as she is, until there is a *stronger* motivation: something that gives her a concrete reason, such as a friend inviting her to share an apartment or a boyfriend who demands more privacy. Some more powerful reason than independence seems to be necessary to motivate Gloria to move out of her mother's home; apparently, desire for independence conflicts with other, stronger motivations for staying—fear of loneliness, fear of trusting her own judgment, unwillingness to make material sacrifices, and sheer inertia.

Motivation, then, does not guarantee the courage to change your life. The motivation must be compared to *other* motivations functioning simultaneously within you and with the other characteristics of courage presented in this chapter. If, in your own decision-making process, you discover that, while you think you have a strong motivation, you still can't seem to take that plunge into the unknown, take a moment to consider other, more subtle motivations operating within you. As the Danish philosopher Søren Kierkegaard has so aptly written, ". . . to venture in the highest sense is precisely to become conscious of oneself." As with all other aspects of good decision-making, understanding your motivations requires a journey into the self.

INTUITION

Courage is very much a matter of intuition. Webster's Dictionary defines intuition as "the immediate knowing or learning of something without the conscious use of reasoning." The psychologist Carl Jung referred to intuition as a *psychic functioning* which we have inherited from our ancestors through our genes. It is that feeling that we "just know" something, without being able to explain how or why.

When we say that we trust our intuitions, we are revealing a basic trust in our own organism. By saying, "My intuition says this is right for me," we are indicating that all of our unconscious and conscious knowledge is converging in a strong feeling of "yes" or "no."

As you go about deciding your life's path, you are probably aware of the interplay between intellectual or logical knowledge and some unexplained "knowing" that also directs you. Whether you choose to explain this in terms of some collective unconscious passed to you genetically from your ancestors (as Jung did); in terms of a direct hookup you have to a Higher Being (as a religionist does); or in terms of the division of the brain into an intuitive right side and a rational left side (as some scientists do), the fact remains that some "gut feelings" are operating along with all your conscious thoughts about changing your life.

When we get past those fears (which you may also experience as "gut feelings" because they seem to reach your very viscera) hampering any desire for change, we begin to experience our intuitions more fully. Somehow those intuitions seem to be connected to the very center of our self and must be reckoned with if we are to feel comfortable with our decisions. In your own life, have you ever had the experience of making a major decision by relying on only the "facts" and what is clearly the most *reasonable* alternative (which usually means the least *demanding* alternative), then feeling somehow flat or disappointed that you left a part of your being unfulfilled, still whispering, "But that's not what I really wanted?" Most likely, that voice was your frustrated intuition, pleading for recognition.

As we pointed out in the second chapter of this book, intuition is a very reliable source of decision-making. Trust in our intuitions helps spark the other elements of courage that, together, spur us into action to change our life.

SENSE OF RESPONSIBILITY

We noted in Chapter Two that one of the major reasons people fail to make changes they desire is unwillingness to assume responsibility. This characteristic is one of the hallmarks of cowardice, just as a sense of responsibility is a hallmark of courage. A courageous person is aware of his responsibility to others as well as to himself; and the strongest responsibility to himself is to understand himself so that he can *freely choose* rather than have his life run by thoughts and emotions he is not even in touch with.

If you will reflect on the courageous decisions you have made in your life—those that called for embracing negative results as well as positive ones—you will find that, in every instance, the sense of *responsibility* was there: a responsibility to act when you felt action was necessary, *because in that very willingness to act, to assume responsibility for your own life, you were affirming the power of your own being.* The courageous person knows that his or her power lies not in "things out there" but in the power of his or her own mind freely to create, to choose, to assume an attitude. When you choose to take responsibility for the course of your own life, you are affirming your primordial instinct to grow, to change, to become. People without this sense of responsibility do not feel compelled to make decisions that demand stretching themselves, that demand saying, "I will do this because I believe in it; I will do it *despite* the negatives I must embrace in order to realize a fuller positivity."

The courageous decision means choosing a life that you consider to be a good life. Though the detailed concept of "a good life" is a little different for each of us, it is difficult to dispute Nietzsche's statement that the good life is the courageous life. No contemporary author has expanded on this statement so eloquently as Dr. Carl Rogers in *On Becoming a Person*:

> The good life is a process, not a state of being. It is a direction, not a destination. The direction which constitutes the good life is that which is selected by the total organism when there is psychological freedom to move in *any* direction. . . . This process of the good life is not, I am convinced, a life for the fainthearted. It involves the stretching and growing of becoming more and more of one's potentialities. It means launching oneself fully into the stream of life. Yet the deeply exciting thing about human beings is that when the individual is inwardly free, he chooses as the good life this process of becoming.

The decision is yours. To make that decision demands the attitude of freedom and the courage to change your life.

Index